CONTEMPORARY
COMPOSERS

THE MACMILLAN COMPANY
NEW YORK · BOSTON · CHICAGO · DALLAS
ATLANTA · SAN FRANCISCO

MACMILLAN & CO., LIMITED
LONDON · BOMBAY · CALCUTTA
MELBOURNE

**THE MACMILLAN COMPANY
OF CANADA, LIMITED**
TORONTO

Vincent d'Indy

CONTEMPORARY COMPOSERS

=

BY

DANIEL GREGORY MASON

AUTHOR OF "BEETHOVEN AND HIS FORERUNNERS," "THE
ROMANTIC COMPOSERS," "FROM GRIEG TO BRAHMS," ETC.

NEW YORK

THE MACMILLAN COMPANY

1929

Norwood Press
J. S. Cushing Co. — Berwick & Smith Co.
Norwood, Mass., U.S.A.

PREFACE

"WE live," wrote Stevenson to Will H. Low in 1884, "in a rum age of music without airs, stories without incident, pictures without beauty, American wood-engravings that should have been etchings, and dry-point etchings that ought to have been mezzo-tints. . . . So long as an artist is on his head, is painting with a flute, or writes with an etcher's needle, or conducts the orchestra with a meat-axe, all is well; and plaudits shower along with roses. But any plain man who tries to follow the obtrusive canons of his art, is but a commonplace figure. . . . He will have his reward, but he will never be thought a person of parts."

What would Stevenson say, I wonder, could he witness the condition to which this confusion of aims, rapidly spreading since he wrote, has now reduced all the arts, and perhaps especially music? "Painting with a flute" hardly sounds fantastic any longer, now that symphonies have given place to symphonic "poems," orchestral "sketches," and tone "pictures," and program music has taken the place of supremacy in the art of tones that magazine illustration occupies among graphic arts. Anyone who tries nowadays to write mere music — expressive of emotion through beauty — is more than ever "a commonplace person." The "persons of parts" are those who give it the quaint local color of folk-songs, like Mr. Percy Grainger; or who make of it an agreeable accessory of dance or stage picture, like Ravel and Strawinsky, or of colored lights and perfumes, like Scriabine; or who spin it into mathematical formulæ as a spider spins web, like Reger; or who use it as a vehicle for *a priori* intellectual theories, like Schoenberg, or as noise for a nerve stimulant, like Mr. Leo Ornstein.

The reader will look in vain for these names, in recent years on everyone's lips, in the table of contents of this book on "Contemporary Composers." In the work of most of them there is, indeed, much of charm or interest, of vividness, perhaps of permanent power. But the time when critical appraisal of them can be anything like final has not yet arrived; and meanwhile there is in their centrifugal tendencies, I believe, a real menace to the best interests of music. One and all, they look away from that inner emotion "to which alone," as Wagner said, "can music give a voice, and music only." They all represent in one way or another that trivializing of the great art, that degradation of it to sensationalism, luxury, or mere illustration, some of the historic causes of which I have tried to suggest in the introduction. No sincere lover of music can regard with anything but the gravest apprehensions such tendencies toward decadence.

Fortunately these are, however, powerfully counteracted, even now, by more constructive forces, carrying forward the evolution of music in and for itself which was the main concern of the great elder masters who regarded it as a supreme emotional language — Bach, Beethoven, Brahms, Wagner, Franck. It is the representatives of this sounder tradition (despite the programmism of Strauss and the sybaritism of Debussy) that I have selected for discussion here. They have also the further advantage of having been long enough before the public to have vindicated already their claims to permanent place in musical history.

The present volume, it may be added, completes the series of studies of great creative musicians from Palestrina to the present day begun in "Beethoven and His Forerunners," "The Romantic Composers," and "From Grieg to Brahms." For permission to reprint the essays it contains, acknowledgment is made to the editors of the *Musical Quarterly*, the *Outlook*, and the *New Music Review*.

D. G. M.

New York,
January 26, 1918.

CONTENTS

LIST OF ILLUSTRATIONS

LIST OF ILLUSTRATIONS

LIST OF ILLUSTRATIONS

I

INTRODUCTION
DEMOCRACY AND MUSIC

—

I

INTRODUCTION
DEMOCRACY AND MUSIC

—

LOVERS and critics of modern music who are at the same time interested students of the social changes which have preceded and accompanied its growth must often ask themselves whether there is any deep connection of cause and effect between the two sets of phenomena, or whether they merely happened to take place at the same time. Have the important social transformations of the nineteenth century reached so far in their influence as to the music of our time? Has sociology any light to throw upon musical art? The question raises a problem as difficult as it is fascinating; and the suggestions which follow are to be taken as guesses and hints, intended to provoke fertile thought, rather than as constituting in any sense a finished theory.

I

The change in the nature of the musical public that has taken place during the nineteenth century has been gradual but far-reaching. The essence of it is expressed by saying that at the end of the eighteenth century music was in the hands of the nobility and gentry, and that at the beginning of the twentieth it is in those of all the people. Under feudal conditions it was organized by the patronage system according to the tastes of the aristocratic few. The thirty most fruitful years of Haydn's life were spent in the employ of Prince Esterhazy; Mozart, a skilled pianist as well as composer, was less dependent on his patron, but his life was probably shortened by the hardships he had to face after he had broken with him; Beethoven, staunch democrat though he was, realized what he owed his four patrons, Archduke Rudolph, and Princes Lobkowitz, Kinsky, and Lichnowsky, and wrote, after the death of some of them had reduced the value of his annuity: "In order to gain time for a great composition, I must always previously scrawl away a good deal for the sake of money. . . . If my salary were not so far reduced as not to be a salary at all, I should write nothing but symphonies . . . and church music, or at most quartets." No doubt the patronage system had its faults and abuses, which have been quite adequately discussed by critics; the fact remains that under it was done the supreme creative work of the golden age of music. Greater than any of its material advantages was the spiritual homogeneity of the group who practised it. By excluding the lower classes, however unjustly, they achieved, though artificially, a unity of feeling that could not then have been achieved otherwise; and as art is in essence an emotional reaction this unity of feeling provided a soil in which its seeds could grow.

But with the French Revolution and the passing of feudalism this old order perished. The proclamation of liberty, equality, and fraternity, paving the way for individualistic competition, introduced the epoch of industrialism and capitalism, in which art, like everything else, was taken out of the hands of a privileged class, and made theoretically accessible to all. As the appreciation of art requires, however, mental and emotional experience, discipline, and refining, a process which takes time, what actually happened was that those gradually emerging from poverty through industrialism — the workers themselves and their children and grandchildren — availed themselves much more slowly and timidly of these spiritual privileges than of the material ones. There remained over from the feudal world a nucleus of cultivated people, sufficiently homogeneous in feeling to retain a standard of taste, sufficiently numerous to exert an influence on production: these were the guardians of the better traditions. They were gradually but steadily interpenetrated and overrun by the emergents, at first in a minority but rapidly becoming the majority, and remaining, of course, unavoidably far more backward in artistic feeling than in economic independence and social ambition. Thus was introduced a formidable cleavage in the musical public, the majority breaking off sharply by their childlike crudity from the more disciplined minority.

The situation was further complicated by the presence of a third class, the idle rich, becoming more numerous under capitalism. It may be doubted whether their attitude towards art was qualitatively different in any important respect from that of the frivolous nobility under feudalism. Both groups regarded music either with complete indifference or else as an amusement, a plaything, a fad; both exercised an influence which through its essential artificiality was potentially perhaps even more baleful than that of the honest crudity of what we have called the emergent class, though actually less disastrous because they were a small minority instead of the majority. But the contribution of this group to the confusion and disorganization characteristic of art under democracy was greater than that of the feudal nobles, because their relation to society as a whole counted more. When they were placed by the emergence of the democratic majority in a vigorous opposition of attitude to the bulk of the people their influence no longer remained largely negative, but made positively for cleavage and disunion. Thus the unity of social emotion on which art so largely depends for a healthy universality was still further disrupted.

We find, then, under democracy, not a fairly homogeneous musical public with emotionally a single point of view, such as existed under feudalism, but a division into a well-meaning but crude majority and two minorities, one cultivated, the other frivolous : all three, but especially the two extremes, held apart by profound differences of feeling. Despite the inevitability and the desirability of democratization as the only path away from slavery, such a disorganization, even if temporary, must evidently, while it lasts, work serious injuries to art. It is worth while to try, taking frankly at first the attitude of the devil's advocate, to trace a few of the more striking of these injuries as they show themselves in contemporary music.

II

Of the "emergents" who constitute the most novel element in the contemporary situation, the well-meaning but crude listeners who form a numerically overwhelming majority of our concertgoers, the effect may be described, in most general terms, as being to put a premium on all that is easily grasped, obvious, primitive, at the expense of the subtler, more highly organized effects of art — on sensation as against thought, on facile sentiment as against deep feeling, on extrinsic association as against intrinsic beauty. Mentally, emotionally, and æsthetically children, they naturally demand the childlike, if not the childish.

There seems to be something far deeper than accident in the coincidence of the rise about 1830, that is, about a generation after the French Revolution, under Berlioz and Liszt, of that program music which is generally acknowledged to be peculiarly characteristic of our period, with the invasion of concert-halls by masses of these childlike listeners, as eager for the stories that music might be made to suggest as they were unprepared to appreciate its more intrinsic beauties. They were drawn by the "program" before they grew up to the "music." Lacking the concentration needed to hold all but the simplest melodies together in their minds, pathetically incapable of the far greater range and precision of attention required to hear synthetically a complex work like an overture or a symphony, they were puzzled or bored by Beethoven, and in their helplessness to follow a musical thread could only grope in the dark until they found a dramatic one. Such a clue in the labyrinth was the "program." They hailed it with the delight of the comparatively unmusical person in opera, who considers it the highest type of music because it supplies him with the largest apparatus of non-musical commentaries (scenery, gestures, words) on the music he cannot understand. Program music, a sort of idealized opera with scenery and actors left to the imagination, fulfilled the same indispensable service for the novice in the concert-room.

The immense popularity of the program idea, from that day to this, is evidence of its complete fitness to the needs of its audience. It s   to them, in effect: "You have little 'ear'   music, and take no more joy in the highly organized melodies of a Beethoven symphony or a Bach fugue, with their infinite subtlety of tonal and rhythmic relationships, than in the most trivial tunes. Never mind: I will give you two or three short motives, clearly labeled, that you cannot help recognizing. This one will mean 'love,' that 'jealousy,' that 'death,' and so on. . . . You are not fascinated by, because you are unable to follow, the creative imagination by which such masters as these build whole worlds of musical beauty out of a few simple themes — an imagination as truly creative as that which carried Newton from the falling apple to the law of gravitation, or directed the infinite patient delving in detail of a Pasteur or a Darwin. Never mind. Remember the story, and you will know that during the love scene the composer must be developing the 'love' motive. . . . You are even more indifferent to the broader balance of part with part, the symmetry and coöperation of all in the whole, harder to grasp just as the concinnity of a Greek temple as a whole is harder to feel than the charm of a bit of sculpture here or the texture of the marble there. Never mind. I will give you a structure in sections, like a sky-scraper. Section will follow section as event follows event in the plot. . . . In short, the story shall be 'All you know, and all you need to know.' It shall be a straw that will keep you from drowning as the inundation of the music passes over you, and that will save you the trouble of learning to swim."

Of course, this does not mean that music of a high order cannot be associated with a program, or that the two cannot be not only coexistent but fruitfully coöperative. They are so in many a representative modern work — in Strauss's "Death and Transfiguration," for instance, or d'Indy's "Istar," or Dukas's "L'Apprenti Sorcier," or Rachmaninoff's "Island of the Dead." What is meant is that the program idea derives both its popularity and its peculiar menace in large measure from the stress it places on the appeal to something outside music — to association, that is — at the expense of the appeal to music itself, and thus from the official sanction it seems to give to what is essentially an unmusical conception of music. The program school of composers is the first school that has not merely tolerated but encouraged, elaborated, and rationalized the conviction of the unmusical that music is to be valued chiefly not for itself, but for something else. How dangerous such a compromise with the majority may be, both to public taste and to the composer, is startlingly, not to say tragically, illustrated by the steady tendency of the greatest master of the school, Richard Strauss, to become more and more trivially "realistic" with each new work, and by the complaisance of the public in paying him vast sums of money for thus progressively corrupting it. In every one of his symphonic poems, from the exuberant "Don Juan" (1888) to the surprisingly banal "Alpensymphonie" (1915), glorious pages of music have alternated with silly tricks of imitation, as for instance the splendid development of the husband theme in the "Symphonia Domestica" with the bawling of the baby; but in the latest we have the maximum of imitation and the minimum of music. Apart from their gorgeous orchestral dress its themes are with few exceptions commonplace, dull, and pretentious. Except in one or two passages they are not imaginatively or significantly developed. On the other hand there is no end of "tone-painting," much of it a revamping of the distant-hunting-horns, rustling-leaves, and warbling-bird-calls which have been time-worn theatrical properties of music ever since Raff's "Im Walde" and Wagner's "Wald-weben"; some of it more original, like the pictures of sunrise and sunset with which the work begins and ends. In these associatively vivid but musically amorphous passages melody, harmony, rhythm, key disappear in a strange opaque cloud of tone, realistically representing night — the kind of night to which the German wit compared Hegel's Absolute — "in which all cows are black." The same childish realism which made Wagner show us his dragon on the stage instead of in our own imaginations introduces a wind-machine in the storm and sheep bells in the mountain pasture. In all this we see an artist who was once capable of writing the introduction and coda of "Death and Transfiguration" taking his art into the nursery to play games with.

But the effect of music on childlike audiences, indisposed to active mental effort and all for taking music passively like a kind of tonal Turkish bath, reaches its logical extreme not in the program music of which Strauss is the most famous exponent, but in that superficially different but fundamentally related movement known as impressionism, which is led by the other most discussed composer of our day, Debussy. Strikingly contrasted as are these two leaders of contemporary music in temperament, in artistic aims, in technical methods, their æsthetic theories are at one in the slight demands they make on the attention of an inevitably inattentive public. Both encourage the listener to look away from the music itself to something that it suggests to him. But impressionism goes further than programmism. May not those people, it says, who find organic melody, development, and form fatiguing, and to whom you give a program to help them out — may they not find the program fatiguing, too? May not its being prescribed offend their sense of "freedom"? Why exact of them the effort to follow even the story? Better to give them simply a title, as vague and elusive as possible, and foster the mood of day-dreaming thus suggested by avoiding all definite melodic, rhythmic, or harmonic features in the music, while enhancing its purely sensuous charm to the utmost degree possible. Such, carried out with extraordinary talent, is the artistic creed of Debussy. Just as programmism appeals from music to association, impressionism appeals to sentiment, to fancy, and to the phantasmagoric reveries upon which they are ever so ready to embark.

It is noteworthy, moreover, that both programmism and impressionism, however systematically they may minimize their demands on the intelligence of their audience, do not abate, but rather tend constantly to increase, their ministration to its sense. Indeed, they systematically maximize their sensuous appeal; and though their characteristic methods of making this appeal differ as widely as their general attitudes, that of programmism being extensive and that of impressionism intensive, the insistence of both on sensuous rather than on intellectual or emotional values is surely one of the most indicative, and it may be added one of the most disquieting, symptoms of the condition of modern music.

The method of the program school in general, and of Strauss in particular, is extensive in that it aims at boundless piling up of means, a formidable accumulation of sonorities for the besieging of the ear. Its motto is that attributed to the German by the witty Frenchman: "Plenty of it." Berlioz, the pioneer of the movement, with his "mammoth orchestras," and his prescription, in his requiem, of four separate brass bands, one at each corner of the church, and eight pairs of kettle-drums in addition to bass drum, gong, and cymbals; Mahler, commencing a symphony with a solo melody for eight horns; Strauss, with his twelve horns behind the scenes in the "Alpensymphonie," to say nothing of wind-machine, thunder-machine, sheep bells, and a whole regiment of more usual instruments — all these disciples of the extensive or quantitative method aim to dazzle, stun, bewilder, and overwhelm. They can be recognized by their abuse of the brass and percussion groups, their childlike faith that if a noise is only loud enough it becomes noble. They have a tendency, too, to mass whole groups of instruments on a single "part," as Tschaikowsky, for instance, so often does with his strings, whatever the sacrifice of interesting detail, for the sake of brilliance and *éclat*. To some extent, of course, all this is justified, even necessitated, by the vast size of modern concert-halls; but a candid observer can hardly deny that it is systematically overdone in the interests of sensationalism. The same tendency is observable also in other than orchestral music. The piano, treated with such admirable restraint by Chopin and by Debussy, has been forced by Liszt and his followers toward jangling, crashing sonorities that can penetrate the most callous sensorium. The equipment of organs with "solo stops" and other devices for the tickling of idle ears has turned the king of instruments too often into a holiday harlequin. Even the string quartet, last rallying-ground of music against the ubiquitous onslaught of sensationalism, begins in many modern scores, with their constant double stops and tremolos, and their "effects" of mutes, pizzicato, "ponticello," "col legno," and the rest, to sound like a rather poor, thin orchestra, striving for a variety and fulness of color beyond its capacity.

The fallacy of the extensive method is that it is trying to satisfy a craving essentially insatiable. Such an appetite for mere quantity of sound grows by what it feeds on; luxury breeds ennui; and, as every sensualist knows to his sorrow, there never can be "plenty of it." A sense of this futility inherent in the extensive method as it has been practised in modern Germany and elsewhere has led another school, chiefly modern French, to try for similar results by a different method, which may be called the intensive. Such a composer as Debussy, who may here be taken as typical, aims, to be sure, primarily at sensuous rather than at mental or spiritual values, but achieves them by qualitative refinement and contrast rather than by quantitative accumulation, and avoids exaggeration in favor of a delicate, almost finical, understatement and suggestiveness. While sonority is as much his god as Strauss's, he is the connoisseur of subtle, elusive sonorities, each to be sipped like a wine of rarest bouquet, rather than an enthusiast of the full-bodied brew. The subtlety of the methods often leads his admirers to claim a superior "spirituality" in the aims, but this is a mistake. His school is more spiritual than Strauss's only as a *gourmet* is more spiritual than a glutton. Both schools prefer sensation to thought and emotion, association to intrinsic beauty, color to line. The difference is that "Pelléas et Mélisande" is the violet or ultraviolet end of the spectrum of which "Salome" is the red.

A curious by-product of the cult of the elusive sonority is the exaggerated, the almost morbid, interest that has emanated from modern France in novelty of harmonic idiom. One would suppose, to read many contemporary critics, that the sole criterion of a good composer depended on his use of some recondite scheme of harmony, whether based on the whole-tone scale, on the mediæval modes, on new applications of chromaticism, on the "harmonic polyphony" of Casella and others, or on the arbitrary asperities of the Italian noise-makers and Mr. Leo Ornstein. If you wish to be considered an "ultra-modernist" you may do quite as you please, both as regards commission and omission, in rhythm, melody, polyphony, form, provided only you are harmonically eccentric. This insistence on harmony, on the momentary tone-combination, suggests a predominant concern with the sensuous side of music which is highly significant as a symptom. It is a stressing of that which the senses alone can perceive from moment to moment, without any aid from memory, imagination, comparison, and other mental acts required for the perception of rhythm and melody. In short, it is an evidence of the same materialistic tendency to rely on the physical rather than the mental appeal, on the investiture of the idea rather than on the idea itself, which we noted in the extensive method. Whatever their differences, both methods are thus at one in the tendency to use materials as makeshifts for thought. Mahler failing to get with eight horns the effect that Schubert got with two — plus a great melodic idea — at the opening of his C Major Symphony, Debussy confectioning a banal bit of tune in muted string or pastoral flute sonorities with piquant harmonies — both are appealing, with varying success, from our minds and hearts to our auditory nerves. The increasing measure of success attending such appeals shows vividly the numerical advantage that the hungry or curious auditory nerves have, in the modern democratic audience, over the enlightened minds and hearts.

III

And indeed, how should we expect it to be otherwise? Enlightened minds and hearts, we must remember, are the finest and rarest fruits of civilization, to be cultivated only under conditions of decent leisure, fair physical and mental health, and free association with "the best that has been done and thought in the world." When they are so rare even in the class that has all these advantages, how shall we expect them to be common among those living either in an industrial servitude that for monotony of toil is almost worse than chattel slavery, or by clerical and other secondary work that through the modern specialization and subdivision of labor condemns each individual to a more or less mechanical repetition of a few small acts through the larger part of his working hours, a routine the relation of which to human life as a whole he often does not see? Writers on sociology are beginning to realize[1] that such conditions of work inevitably produce a morbid psychological condition in the worker, dulling his mind by the meaningless drudgery and depressing his body and nerves by fatigue-poisons, so that even in his few hours of leisure his perfectly natural seeking for pleasure does not take entirely normal paths. Too exhausted to respond to delicate shades and subtle relationships, whether in sensuous or mental objects, his jaded nerves cry out for violent stimuli, for sharp contrasts, for something to goad and

[1] See, for example, "The Great Society," by Graham Wallas, and "Work and Wealth," by J. A. Hobson.

whip them into new activity. This craving for violent stimuli is the essential feature of the fatigue-psychology. Now, is it not highly suggestive that the age of industrialism is also the age of a hundred goads for tired nerves — of the newspaper headline, the dime-novel and "penny-thriller," the lurid moving-picture drama, rag-time and the "revue"? And is it not possible that the sensationalism of so much modern music is only another evidence, on a somewhat higher plane, of the working of this same psychology of fatigue?

Again, these overworn nerves of ours have within a comparatively short period had brought to bear upon them, through the progress of modern invention with its cheap printing, quick transportation, and long distance communication, a thousand distractions. No longer insulated from the outlying world, so to speak, by time and space, as were our more simply-living ancestors, we read, hear, and see as much in a day as they did in a week. The inevitable result has been a diffusion of attention fatal to concentrated thought except for the most resolute, breeding in the average man mental indigestion and habits of disorder and impatience, and gradually evolving the characteristic modern type — quick, sharp, and shallow. Outward distraction has thus added its influence to inner weariness to urge our art away from quiet thought towards ever noisier solicitation. For thought always depends on simplification, on inhibition: in order to think we must neglect the given-by-sense, as we see strikingly in the case of the absent-minded, in order to attend to the given-by-memory-and-imagination; and over-stimulation of sense is therefore just as hostile to thought as the depression of the higher mental faculties through fatigue. Thus it is highly characteristic of our prevailing attitude that we strive, not for elimination, but for accumulation, distraction, dissipation. The formula is always mental apathy, physical and nervous excitement. Not having the joy of the mastery which comes only through thought, because we lack both concentration and favorable opportunity to discipline ourselves, we seek the stimulus of constant change. We digest nothing, taste everything; "eclecticism" is our euphemism for spreading our attention very wide and very thin; and the nightmare that you soon uncover under all our art is not that our minds may become bewildered (for that they are already), but that our senses may become jaded — which of course they do.

Still another line of influence that may be traced from general modern conditions to the peculiar qualities of modern art concerns especially the third of the classes described above, the capitalist class. Here again we find a morbid condition, a distortion of wholesome human contacts; but here instead of the impediment of meaningless drudgery, it is the incubus of a fruitless, selfish idleness. Cut off from the normal outlet of energy in useful work, the luxurious classes become pampered and bored, and develop through very vacuity a perverted taste for the unusual, the queer, the generally upside down and backside to. Every season sees a new crop of the "isms" thus produced, the ephemera of the world of art, which live a day and die as soon as they lose their one interest, novelty. Of all manifestations of so-called "art" they are the most sterile, the most completely devoid of vital relation to any real impulse. They might be ignored did they not complicate still further an already complicated situation, and were they not an additional, though a largely negative, illustration of the close causative relation between general social conditions and artistic expression that our discussion is making more and more evident. Fortunately they produce little enduring effect beyond their own narrow circles; for as they spring not from any vital interest, but only from an unguided curiosity and desire for excitement, they take mutually opposing forms and largely cancel each other. Thus, for instance, fads for very old or for very new music, directed as they are toward the mere age or the mere newness, and having no concern with the quality of the music itself, leave the actual public taste just where it would have been had they never arisen. Nevertheless the diversion of so much energy, which might under better conditions find an outlet in fruitful activity, to a sterile posture-making, is uneconomical and to be regretted.

So far, we have been looking chiefly, from

the point of view of the devil's advocate, at
the injurious influences on contemporary music
that can be traced with some degree of plausi-
bility to the capitalistic and industrial social
system of the nineteenth century. Noting
the sensational bent, whether extensively or
intensively expressing itself, of the chief contemporary schools, we have asked ourselves
whether it could be attributed in some measure
to the kind of demand made by an audience
dulled by overwork at monotonous tasks and
depressed by fatigue-poisons. Remarking the
multiplicity of fads and "isms" by which our
art is confused, we have asked how far these
might be attributed to the cravings of a group
whose normal appetites have been perverted
by luxury and self-centered isolation. All of
these evils, we have insisted, are aggravated
in their effects by the distractions under which
we live. It is now time, however, taking a
more positive view and attempting a more
constructive theory, to ask how these evils
may be combated, what more hopeful elements already exist in the situation, and what
others may be expected to develop in the future.

IV

First of all, it may be suggested that, so far as these evils are fairly attributable to the social conditions of the nineteenth century, they may fairly be expected to be mitigated somewhat by those changes which already seem probable in those of the twentieth. The capitalistic era seems likely to be followed by an era of coöperation or communism; and in countless ways such a change must eventually be deeply revivifying to all forms of art. Of course, it is only too easy to indulge in baseless dreams of the results upon art of a millennium brought about in this way, only too easy to forget that we are only at the threshold of such new systems of organization, and that they may go the wrong way instead of the right. All we can safely say is that if they do go the right way they will rescue art, among many other human interests, from the condition to which much of it has been prostituted under capitalism.

Let us suppose, for instance, that something like what Mr. H. G. Wells calls the Great

29

State [1] eventually results from the troublous reconstructions through which we are living. The Great State is only one of three possibilities he sees in the further adjustment of the leisure class and the labor class of our present order. The first possibility (and a disagreeably vivid one it must seem to all thoughtful Americans) is that "the leisure class may degenerate into a waster class," and the labor class "may degenerate into a sweated, overworked, violently resentful and destructive rebel class," and that a social *débâcle* may result. The second possibility is that the leisure class "may become a Governing Class (with waster elements) in an unprogressive Bureaucratic Servile State," in which the other class appears as a "controlled, regimented, and disciplined Labour Class." The third possibility is that the leisure class "may become the whole community of the Great State, working under various motives and inducements, but not constantly, nor permanently, nor unwillingly," while the labor class is

[1] "Social Forces in England and America," by H. G. Wells, New York and London, 1914.

"rendered needless by a general labour conscription, together with a scientific organization of production, and so re-absorbed by re-endowment into the Leisure Class of the Great State."

The first two of these possible conditions would be fatal to art, one through anarchy and loss of standards, the other through conventionalization. The third would bring about a renascence, after a troubled period of conflicting standards and of readjustments such as we find ourselves in to-day. The main elements in such a progress would be, first, the gradual refining, deepening, and vitalizing of the taste of the general public under the influence of increasing leisure, health, self-respect, and education; second, the cutting off of extravagance, luxury, and faddism in the wealthier classes by a wholesome pressure of enforced economy; third, increasing solidarity of feeling in the whole social fabric through such a mutual *rapprochement*, giving the indispensable emotional basis for vital art.

There are already some encouraging evidences of such developments. Much preparatory work towards the formation of better standards of public taste has been unobtrusively done, at least in our larger cities, by free lectures and cheap recitals and concerts. Two disadvantages, however, have often attended such work, reducing its benefits. One has come from the common fallacy that what is done for the many must be done so as to please the many — a view often supposed to be "democratic." Emerson was more truly democratic when he told us to "cease this idle prating about the masses," and set about extracting individuals from them; for real democracy never forgets that the majority are always inferior, and its aim must be to give the superior minority a chance to make their influence felt. In other words, to level down to the people is to vulgarize rather than to popularize. Theodore Thomas set a model for the conductor of popular concerts in the best sense, for all time, when he replied to one of his orchestra players who said that people did not like Wagner: "Then we must play him until they do."

The second disadvantage is even harder to avoid, even for administrators of the highest standards, because it seems to be almost intrinsic in this kind of work. It comes from the passive nature of the people's participation. Giving even the best concerts seems often too much like handing the people music at the end of a stick — "Take it or leave it"; naturally, having so little choice in its selection, they often leave it; and even when they try their best to take it, they cannot get so much out of it as if they were actively helping to produce it. This is the reason that more active forms of music-making, even if crude, like the music school settlement work and the community choruses that have been making such strides in recent years, seem so full of promise. The singing in the public schools, too, would have done far more than it has, had not the standards been debased, as Mr. T. W. Surette has ably shown,[1] to the childish tastes, not of the children themselves, who could appreciate better things, but of their dull and routine-enslaved elders. Yet here again we must beware of a too easy optimism.

[1] In an article on Public-School Music, Atlantic Monthly, December, 1916.

There is no magic about the community chorus that can suddenly change bad taste to good. Too often we seem here, as in all other activities for popularizing music, to oscillate helplessly between two evils. On the one hand is the crudity of actual taste: the majority prefer rag-time and the musical comedies to folk-songs or the simple classics. On the other hand is the apathy that comes of prescriptions from outsiders: musical activity that is not spontaneous is sterile. Progress seems to come painfully and uncertainly from a constant zigzagging between these two evils, getting gradually away from them as the taste of the minority exercises its persuasiveness.

As for the wealthier classes, it must be confessed that there are so far few evidences of any permanent displacement of luxury and artificiality by saner and simpler tastes. Yet there are even here one or two hopeful signs, of which the most conspicuous is the recent enthusiasm for folk-songs. This is rather too good to be altogether true. It is hard to believe in the complete sincerity of those who go into the same rhapsodies over a perfectly

34

simple and rather crude peasant song that a year or two ago they reserved for the exquisite day-dreams of Debussy or the exotic inconsequentialities of Cyril Scott. Moreover, the appreciation of folk-song, though a normal and indeed indispensable stage in musical education, is only the very first phase of initiation to the deeper and subtler beauties of musical art, and not a stage to be dwelt in with complacency. Yet so far as it goes, and in the measure of its sincerity, the interest in folk-song is of good augury. It means concern with melody, always and everywhere the soul of music, rather than with externalities like orchestral color, or harmonic "effects," or quasi-poetic associations and programs. It means sympathy with simple and broadly human, universal emotions, such as inspire the greatest as well as such primitive music. It may mean the beginning of a real and eventually a developed taste for good music. And it is a good foundation for such a *rapprochement* of all classes of music-lovers as may come, we may hope, with the coming of the Great State.

If our cursory examination of the general tendencies of our day reveals no striking preponderance of good over bad, shows us no movement of any majority that we can acclaim without qualification, we may now remind ourselves for our comfort that this has always been the case in all times, and that there is indeed a curious illusion, resolvable only by close scrutiny, that makes our own time seem worse to us, in comparison with others, than it really is. We have to remember that the baser elements of our own time make a much greater impression on us, in relation to the finer ones, than those of the past. A living fool can make as much noise as a wise man (if not far more); a dead one is silent forever. The gold of Beethoven's day, of which he was himself the purest nugget, comes down to us bright and untarnished, so that we forget all the dross that has been thrown on the scrap-heap of time. Our own gold is almost hidden from us by the glitter of the tinsel.

"The world of music," says Sir Charles Stanford,[1] "is not substantially different from

[1] "Pages from an Unwritten Diary," C. V. Stanford.

what it has been. It has always exalted those of its contemporary composers who dealt in frills and furbelows above those who considered the body more important than its clothes. Only a few wise heads knew of the existence of Bach. Rossini was rated by the mass of the public far higher than Weber, Spohr than Beethoven, Meyerbeer than Wagner. Simrock said that he made Böhm pay for Brahms."

It is always necessary to wait for the winnowing process of time before we can see the true proportions of an age. Hence we can never see our own age in its true proportions, and since the second- and third-rate elements in it are ever more acclaimed by the majority than the first-rate, we always see it worse than it is. We live, so to speak, in the glare of noon-day, and cannot see the true coloring of our world, which will appear only at evening. Hence in every age the tragi-comedy is repeated of acclaiming the mediocre and the meretricious, and ignoring worth. The Gounods always patronize the Francks. The answer of philosophy is Emerson's:

"Ideas impregnable: numbers are nothing. Who knows what was the population of Jerusalem? 'Tis of no importance whatever. We know that the Saint and a handful of people held their great thoughts to the death; and the mob resisted and killed him; and, at the hour, fancied they were up and he was down; when, at that very moment, the fact was the reverse. The principles triumphed and had begun to penetrate the world. And 'tis never of any account how many or how rich people resist a thought."

Our final question, then, resolves itself to this: Are there in the music of our day, known or unknown to the majority, any such vital "thoughts," based on principles that a discerning criticism may see even now to have "triumphed and begun to penetrate the world"? Is there music being written to-day which is modern, not through its pampering to jaded sense or dulled intelligence, but through its intuition and expression of the deeper emotional experience and spiritual aspiration of our time? Is there music, in short, not only seductive to the ear but beautiful to the mind?

To answer such a question intelligently we shall have to take account of certain truths which the foregoing discussion has tended to establish, and which may now be made explicit. Thought, emotion, all that we call the spiritual side of music, expresses itself not through sonorous or harmonic effects, primarily sensuous in appeal, but through melody and rhythm and their interplay and elaboration in so-called thematic development. In truly great music we remember, not such and such a bit of tone-color, not this or that sonority, but the soaring or tender curve of the themes, their logical yet ever new unfolding, their embodiment, in the whole composition, of richest variety with completest final unity. The man in the street is absolutely right in feeling that music succeeds or fails by its tunes; his limitation arises in his conception of "tune."

Again, since the creation and manipulation of great "tunes" or themes, unlike the hitting off of sonorous effects or the discovery of *rococo* harmonies, comes never by luck, but only through a discipline based on the assimilation of all that is best in music, we always find that all really fine music is firmly founded upon tradition, and reaches its roots into the past, while blossoming, so to speak, into the future. The artist, despite the popular sup-position to the contrary, depends on his fore-runners quite as closely as the scientist. You can no more write a solid sonata without know-ing Beethoven than you can work efficiently in biology in ignorance of Darwin. Yet on the other hand this assimilation of the past has to produce, not an academic and sterile complacency with what is, but an equipped and curious advance upon what is to be: the artist, like the scientist, brings all his learning to the test in acts of creative imagination, leaps in the dark. Thus artistic advance may be figured as like the shooting of frost crystals on a window pane; never is there a crystal that is not firmly attached by traceable lines to the main body; yet no one can prophesy whither each fine filament may strike out in its individual adventure. The great artist is bound to the past by love and docility, to the future by a faith that overleaps convention.

Looked at in the light of these considerations,

contemporary music presents a scheme of light and shade somewhat different from that ordinarily accepted. If some high lights are overshadowed, others seem to shine more brightly. There is plenty of hopeful promise for the future. Leaving aside the sounder elements in Strauss and Debussy, in whom there is so much of the richness of decay, we shall find the chief centers of truly creative activity perhaps in three composers who in their differing ways and degrees carry on the great tradition: Rachmaninoff in Russia, Elgar in England, and d'Indy in France. Each of these men reaches back roots to the primal sources of musical life — Bach and Beethoven: Rachmaninoff through Tschaikowsky, the eclectic Elgar through Mendelssohn, Brahms, Wagner, and others, and d'Indy through Wagner and Franck. Each, as we see in such modern classics as "Toteninsel," the A flat Symphony, and "Istar," can create, in settings of modern opulence of color, nobly beautiful forms, melodies that live and soar in a spiritual heaven. All, too, though in varying degrees, move on as creators should toward the unknown. Here the Frenchman has perhaps, with his characteristic lucidity and logic, something the advantage of the more sensuous Slav and the more convention-beset Anglo-Saxon. Rachmaninoff, for all his warmth, does not always escape the vulgarity of Tschaikowsky, and Elgar cannot always forget the formulæ of oratorio. But in d'Indy, with his untrammeled experimental attitude toward all modern possibilities, we have an influence destined steadily to grow and already clearly suggesting an epoch combining the best of the old ways with new ones at which we can for the present only guess.

II
RICHARD STRAUSS

—

RICHARD STRAUSS

—

I

THE chronology of Richard Strauss's artistic life up to the present time arranges itself almost irresistibly in the traditional three periods, albeit in his case the philosophy of these periods has to be rather different from that, say, of Beethoven's. "Discipline, maturity, eccentricity," we say with sufficient accuracy in describing Beethoven's development. The same formula for Strauss will perhaps be tempting to those for whom the perverse element in the Salome-Elektra period is the most striking one; but it is safer to say simply: "Music, program music, and music drama." Born in 1864, he produced during his student years, up to 1886, a great quantity of well-made and to some extent personal music, obviously influenced by Mendelssohn, Schumann, and Brahms, and com-

45

prising sonatas, quartets, concertos, and a symphony. He himself has told how he then came under the influence of Alexander Ritter, and through him of Wagner, Berlioz, and Liszt; how this influence toward "the poetic, the expressive, in music" acted upon him "like a storm wind"; and how the "Aus Italien," written in 1886, is the connecting link between his earlier work and the series of symphonic poems that follows in the second period. The chief titles and dates of this remarkable series may be itemized here: "Macbeth," 1886-7; "Don Juan," 1888; "Tod und Verklärung," 1889; "Till Eulenspiegel" and "Also Sprach Zarathustra," 1894; "Don Quixote," 1897; "Ein Heldenleben," 1898; and the "Symphonia Domestica," 1903. The period of program music, containing also, of course, other works such as the operas "Guntram" and "Feuersnot," innumerable songs, and a violin sonata strayed from the first period, thus lasts from his twenty-second to his thirty-ninth year. Since then Strauss has devoted himself chiefly to works for the stage, comprising "Salome" (1906), "Elektra" (1908),

"Der Rosenkavalier" (1911), "Ariadne auf Naxos," (1913), and "Josephs Legende" (1914). His latest work is again in the province of instrumental music — an "Alpine Symphony."

This rapid survey of Strauss's creative activity shows that the natural bent of his mind is toward the realistic and dramatic side of his art; it was only in his youth, before he had found himself, that he wrote self-sufficing music; and though lyrical power is shown in many of his songs and in passages of almost all the orchestral works, yet it is on the whole true to say that the essential Strauss is Strauss the dramatist. And if we ask ourselves what are the qualities of temperament requisite to a dramatist, we shall find in Strauss's possession of them in altogether unusual measure the key to his commanding position among the musico-dramatists of our day.

These qualities are the same for a dramatic artist who works in tones as for one who works in words. First of all he must be a man of keen observation, of penetrating intelligence, able to note all that passes about him and to interpret it with something of cold scientific precision. He must be able to seize human types and divine human motives quite different from his own, as they are objectively. He must resist distorting them by reading into them his own impulses and sentiments, as a man of more subjective temperament and less critical detachment always does. In short, he must be of the active rather than the contemplative type, and have a good measure of that faculty of impersonal intellectual curiosity which gives a Shakespeare his supreme power of objective observation.

But though he must not distort others by viewing them through himself, he must nevertheless interpret them through reference to his own feelings, since these are the only feelings with which he is directly acquainted. That is to say, he must be able to place himself, by sympathetic imagination, at the points of view of those he studies. Such sympathetic imagination is so very different a thing from subjective distortion that without it no real understanding of one's fellows is possible at all. The great dramatist needs, then, deep and rich emotion, quite as much as the lyric singer — but emotion ever guided by the sympathy which brings it into play. It is this emotion, guided by sympathetic imagination, that gives the very aspect of life, and its power to move us, to the creation that mere intellectual observation alone could never vitalize.

And finally, the dramatic artist, besides observing keenly and interpreting sympathetically, must view all that he sees with a certain magnanimous many-sidedness, a sort of sweet and mellow wisdom, which is hard to describe but unmistakable when encountered. We find it in all really great creative artists, who seem to view life not only keenly, not only sympathetically, but also wisely and as if from above, from that vantage point of a wider insight than that of any of their subjects, so that in their summing up of them they are able to set them in proper relation one to another, and by so doing to get a true and calm picture of human life as a whole. This power of philosophic or poetic vision, this magnanimity, we instinctively demand of the artist. It satisfies a fundamental human craving. The moral in the fable is a naïve embodiment of it; it comes even into the uncongenial atmosphere of the light comedy of manners in the rhymed epilogue; its musical incarnation we find in many of the quiet codas of Brahms, or in the thoughtful "Der Dichter spricht" at the end of Schumann's "Kinderscenen."

The object of the present essay is to show that Strauss has, in unequal but high degree, these qualities of the dramatist: observation, sympathy, and magnanimity. The first he has in almost unparalleled measure; the second somewhat fitfully, sometimes inhibited by his ironic cynicism; the third in his most genial moods, as for instance, in the epilogue to "Till Eulenspiegel," but not when misled by over-realistic aims. The evidence of his possession of these qualities that we shall especially look for will be not that afforded by his acts or his sayings, but rather the irrefragable testimony of his musical works themselves.

II

Since a man's temperament is what ultimately determines the peculiar combination

of qualities making up his artistic individuality
— his characteristic powers and shortcomings
— the first questions we have to ask ourselves
regarding any artist we propose to study will
always be: "What is his temperament?"
"To which of the two great types does it belong, the active or the contemplative?" "Does
its power lie primarily in observation or in introspection?" "Does it impel him towards
objective characterization or toward the utterance of subjective feeling?" Elsewhere,
in studying these antitheses of temperament
in particular cases, such as those of Mendelssohn and Schumann,[1] and of Saint-Saëns
and Franck,[2] occasion has been taken to discuss
in some detail the rationale of their musical expression. At present our interest is in finding in Strauss a rather extreme case of the
active temperament, a man of positively ex-
plosive nervous energy.

It is only necessary to assemble a few of his
characteristic melodic motives to see that this
energy naturally translates itself, melodically,

[1] See especially "The Romantic Composers."
[2] In the essays on these composers in "From Grieg to Brahms."

into wide erratic skips and incisive abrupt rhythms. Here are a few of them:

FIGURE I.

(a) From "Till Eulenspiegel."

(b) From "Don Juan."

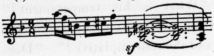

(c) From "Ein Heldenleben."

(d) From "Also Sprach Zarathustra."

(e) From the "Symphonia Domestica."

The chief theme of the arch mischief-maker, "Till Eulenspiegel," is necessarily capricious, but it is doubtful if even for him anyone but Strauss would have thought of those surprising jumps, landing each time on an unexpected note. In the main theme of "Don Juan" we have a good example of his rhythmic energy. Note the variety of the figures: the sixteenth notes in the first measure, swarming up to the high E; the still further ascending triplet; the even more incisive dotted group leading to the emphatic half notes. In similar general style is the chief theme of "Ein Heldenleben," depicting the hero, but less lithe, more burly and almost awkwardly powerful. The theme of "great longing" from "Also Sprach Zarathustra" conveys its impression through the wide jumps, covering almost three octaves in two vigorous dashes. The theme of "the Wife," from the "Symphonia Domestica," illustrates Strauss's love of turning the unexpected way. Notice the downward jump of a ninth, and the cadence transferred to a higher octave than we expect.

The same story of overflowing nervous energy is told by two other characteristics of Strauss's melody. Like all sanguine natures he has more rising than falling phrases. The buoyancy of (*b*), (*c*), and (*d*) in Figure I is irrepressible; (*a*) has a falling curve, somewhat coy; (*e*) begins in the same wheedling vein, but ends with a rise of self-confident energy. A canvass of all the motives in the symphonic poems would probably demonstrate that seventy-five per cent of them rise in pitch. The second peculiarity is more subtle but even more significant — a preference for "rising" or anacrustic rhythms, culminating in an accented final note after several unaccented ones, to "falling" or thetic rhythms beginning with the heavy part of the measure. The elasticity of the rising rhythm is clearly shown in all the excerpts of Figure I except that from "Ein Heldenleben"; that, naturally, begins doggedly on the down beat. Only a systematic study can show the extent of Strauss's addiction to the rising rhythm.

These considerations, to which might perhaps be added his preference for the major to the minor mode, and for the vigorous duple to the more subtle triple meter, afford us quite ample internal evidence of his belonging to the temperamental type of the actives, like Mendelssohn and Saint-Saëns (however he may differ from them musically) rather than to that of the contemplatives, — the Schumanns and the Francks. To these positive points we might add negative ones, dealing with his emotional shortcomings. This, indeed, we shall have to do later, in the interest of a just critical estimate; but for the present it will be better worth while to examine the positive results, in the way of keen observation and masterly characterization, of this active-minded interest of Strauss in what lies about him.

III

Strauss's characterization is consummate. Superlatives are dangerous, but probably no other musician has ever carried to such a point the power of music to depict, or at least, to suggest, varieties of character, both in human beings and in inanimate objects. Strauss's reported remark that music was becoming so definite that we should soon be able to portray a tablespoon so unmistakably that it could be told from the rest of the silverware is probably an instance of his sardonic delight in hoaxing the public; but if anyone is going to subject the art of tones to this curious test, we are all agreed, doubtless, that it should be Strauss himself. Meanwhile, failing a tablespoon, we have a sufficiently varied collection of portraits in his gallery, each sketched with a Sargent-like penetration.

We have seen, for example, in Figure I*a*, Till Eulenspiegel the arch mischief-maker, irrepressible, incorrigible. Here, on the other hand, is Till sentimental, making love to a village maiden, his original insolence tamed into a simpering persuasiveness, his theme, at first so galvanic, now languishing in its plaintive downward droopings (Figure II, page 57). Later we see him, repulsed by the maiden, storming in ungovernable fury.[1]

Here, again, belonging to a quite other world, is Don Quixote, "the knight of the sorrowful

---

[1] The passage, page 13 of the two-hand piano arrangement, page 26 of the orchestra score, is too long to quote here.

FIGURE II.

"Till" in love.

FIGURE III.

Don Quixote, the knight of the sorrowful visage.

visage," aging and broken, yet full of chivalrous and idealistic notions, and thus at once inspiring and pathetic (Figure III, page 57). What a contrast is his rascal of a servant, Sancho Panza, good-natured and irresponsible, sauntering through life with a minimum of effort and a maximum of diversion:

FIGURE IV.

Sancho Panza.

We find a somewhat similar principle of contrast, though between very different types of character, in the themes of the husband and the wife in the "Symphonia Domestica." The latter has been cited at Figure I*e*. Its suggestion of coy graciousness and feminine charm is due in part to the tender downward inflections of the opening figure, and partly to the anacrustic rhythm (beginning with unaccented notes). The theme of the husband, with which the work opens, starts out with an "inversion" of this three-note figure of the wife: the motives complementary to each other, so to speak, as if Strauss had wished to suggest the reciprocal relation of marriage. Yet the rising inflection and the falling rhythm of the husband version give it a vigor that completely differentiates it from the other, even if we ignore for the moment the effect of the contrasting keys of F major and B major, a matter of which we shall have more to say presently.

The subtlety of the composer's use of rhythm for characterization can hardly be exaggerated. It almost justifies the extreme detail of his annotator's analyses, as for example of Mr. Wilhelm Klatte's diagnosis of the hero's character in "Ein Heldenleben." This reads like an old-fashioned phrenological chart. Mr. Klatte finds in his hero "a genial nature, emotional and vibratory" (measures 1–6 and 9–12 of the opening theme), a "haughty and firm step" (measures 6–8), and an "indomitable will" (measures 13–16). Furthermore the continuation in B major and A flat, Mr. Klatte tells us, shows that the paragon has "richness of fantasy, warmth and elasticity of feeling, allied with lightness of movement — whose tendency is always toward buoyancy and onward and upward effort, thus imparting an effect of inflexible and well-directed determination instead of low-spirited or sullen obstinacy." Mr. Klatte makes a considerable demand on our powers of credence. Yet we must be reluctant to place limits to a power of rhythmo-melodic suggestion that can give us such extremes of opposed character as the naïve innocence of the "Childhood" motive in "Tod und Verklärung," and the degenerate superstition and pathological fear of Herodias, with her eerie whole-tone scale, in "Salome."

Highly characteristic of Strauss, both in its subtle use of rhythmo-melodic characterization and in the rather malicious quality of its humor, is the "Science" section in "Also Sprach Zarathustra." This powerful if over-ambitious work deals with a matter that can hardly be put into music, even by Strauss: with the opposition, namely, between the Christian ideal of self-abnegation and Nietzsche's philosophy of self-fulfilment. In this particular section of it Strauss is trying to suggest the dustiness, mustiness, and inconclusiveness of "Science" from the standpoint of the passions; this he does by making a frightfully complicated fugue from his main theme. How slyly does he here satirize science! How to the life does his fugue theme, starting off boldly in C major and square-cut rhythm, and presently wandering into chromatic harmonies and indecisive triplets, symbolize the initial arrogance and final futility of scholastic systems!

Figure V.

"Of Science." Fugue theme from "Also Sprach Zarathustra."

In the use of harmony for characterization Strauss is no less skilful than in the more important matters of melody and rhythm. The essential quality of his harmony is perhaps less "ultra-modern" than is sometimes supposed. In spite of the sensational innovations of "Salome" and "Elektra," he is so intensely German in feeling and so well founded on the German classics that the nucleus of his harmonic system is the diatonic scale, simple and rugged. One thinks of such powerful themes as that of "Transfiguration" or the "Hero" as the essential Strauss. Even "Salome" has its Jochanaan, and the "Symphonia Domestica" is surprisingly diatonic. Strauss is more nearly related to the virile Wagner of "Die Meistersinger" than to that other more sensuous Wagner of "Tristan und Isolde." Of course, there are wondrously expressive chromatic passages in Strauss, as for instance the "Grablied" in "Zarathustra"; but on the whole his musical foundation is tonic-and-dominant, like Mozart's, Beethoven's, and Brahms's.

It is in the boldly imaginative and unconventional arrangement of simple material that Strauss gets his most striking harmonic effects. Plain "triads" and "dominant sevenths," the small musical change of hack composers, turn to gold in his hands. The touchingly expressive cadence of Don Quixote's theme will illustrate. The material is of the

FIGURE VI.

Cadence from "Don Quixote."

most ordinary, yet the effect is magical and its dramatic appropriateness surprising. In the words of Mr. Arthur Kahn,[1] "These confused harmonic windings through which the central chords of the previously established key are reached, characterize strikingly the well-known tendency of Don Quixote towards false conclusions. He goes carefully out of the way of natural sequences and pal-

[1] Don Quixote, erläutert von Arthur Kahn, Der Musikführer no. 148, Leipzig.

pable facts, in order not to demolish therewith his fancy structures."

Strauss has carried this principle of the close juxtaposition of chords more or less foreign to each other, and even of different keys, to greater and greater lengths in his more recent works, and to the effects of "queerness" which result when these foreign tonal groups quickly follow each other, and of more or less extreme dissonance when they occur simultaneously, he owes much of the violently adverse criticism to which he has been subjected. Indeed, nothing has more retarded his general acceptance than these abrupt transitions and unaccustomed discordancies. The matter is of sufficient importance to intelligent appreciation of him to justify a brief digression here. For any composer who conceives music as a number of melodies proceeding together in greater or less amity, but preserving the measure of independence that individuality and vigorous movement demand — and Strauss is to a peculiar degree such a polyphonic composer — a certain amount of physical harshness at moments when the melodies happen to clash is not only unavoidable but positively desirable, as tending to throw each into relief. According to the degree of his experience the listener follows the composer in this respect: that is, he accepts with something more than passive endurance, yes, with active pleasure, the physically disagreeable clashes (dissonances) which by setting off the differing contours of the melodies emphasize for him their mental and emotional appeal; but not — and the point is of prime importance to the would-be music-lover — not if he does not follow the melodies, that is, not if he cannot hear consecutively as well as moment by moment — for it is only by following the threads, so to speak, that we can untangle the knots. Accordingly most untrained listeners dislike, probably, music that contains many of these knots, the presence of which makes it so interesting and exciting to the experienced ear. The woman who confessed to her piano teacher that she did not like Bach's Two-part Inventions because they were so "ugly" was not less cultivated but only more frank than many who have not discovered that Bach has to be heard "horizontally" (to borrow a figure from musical notation) rather than "vertically."

This gift of horizontal hearing is peculiarly necessary to anyone who would disentangle the tonal knots in which Strauss delights, working as he does with many more than two voices and with the vast fund of harmonic possibilities accumulated since Bach's day to draw upon. And he is not the man to use his resources timidly, or to make any concessions to laziness or inexperience in his listeners. Here is a reduction of a passage from "Ein Heldenleben" to its essential elements.

FIGURE VII.

The heavy brass gives the foundation harmonies; the strings and woodwind have an
upward-moving melody, and the eight horns
blare forth at the same time a slower-moving
downward melody. If we read almost any
single chord vertically, we shall find it has its
measure of harshness, sometimes considerable.
If we listen to the coherent voices, none of
these dissonances will trouble us in the least.
This is a very simple example of what Strauss
is constantly doing in a far more complex way.[1]

It is a real difficulty in the way of Strauss
appreciation that while only familiarity can
enable us to follow the intricate windings
of the threads that make up his gorgeously
rich fabrics, frequent hearings of his later
and more complex symphonic poems are not
to be had, even in the large cities. In the meanwhile we have no recourse but piano arrangements, unsatisfactory for two reasons. In the

[1] The jump of the horns in the fourth measure illustrates another obstacle to understanding that the inexperienced listener
often meets in Strauss. He is quite careless as to what register,
high or low, the "resolutions" of his dissonances occur in; they
jump about from octave to octave; and the hearer, to follow
them, has to be equally agile.

first place, it is physically impossible to play with two hands even a respectable fraction of the melodies that Strauss delights to elaborate for two hundred; and four-hand versions are better only in degree, not in kind. Secondly, piano versions fail us precisely in this matter of unraveling dissonance, since by reducing a colored pattern to monochrome they diminish the salience of the lines we are trying to follow, and by juxtaposing in one tone-quality tones that in the orchestra are softened by difference of timbre they notably increase the physical harshness of the combinations. Obviously, then, we must be exceedingly chary of condemning Strauss, or any other composer, for orchestral dissonance that we have either become acquainted with insufficiently, or only through piano arrangements.

After making these subtractions, however, there undoubtedly remain many puzzling clashes of tone in Strauss's scores, which can be accounted for only as introduced either for color or for dramatic expression. The use of dissonance for the sake of color enrichment is a familiar proceeding in modern music, especially in that of impressionistic type like Debussy's and Ravel's. Such use is essentially decorative. To a more or less clearly defined harmonic nucleus are added softer tones, clashing with it, and thus forming about it an aura or atmosphere elsewhere compared to the mist which softens the outlines of the landscape.[1] Strauss is too fond of clear outlines and solid mass to employ these impressionistic methods habitually, or even frequently; but when he does, it is with his usual skill and daring. The theme of the silver rose in "Der Rosenkavalier" is the inevitable example: the last pages of the score are crowded with those silvery, scarcely audible triads of celesta and flutes, shifting and settling on the stronger G major chord like snowflakes on a leaf (Figure VIII, page 70).

Delicious as are these shimmerings, a use of dissonance on the whole more characteristic of the masculine nature of Strauss is the harsher, more insistent juxtaposition of clashing tones for the sake of their potency in the expression

[1] Essay on Chopin, in "The Romantic Composers."

FIGURE VIII.

The silver rose motive, from "Der Rosenkavalier."

of the tragic, the gruesome, or the abnormal. Naturally this is pushed furthest in the treatment of such pathological subjects as "Salome" and "Elektra," where its effect is carefully enhanced by contrast with strong or clear consonant harmonies — "Salome" has its Jochanaan and "Elektra" its Chrysothemis. The close juxtaposition of foreign tone groups, either successive or simultaneous, is carried to great lengths in these operas. The theme of the chattering Jews in "Salome" is an example of the successive, as is the curious succession

of the chords of F minor and B minor at Chrysothemis' entrance in "Elektra." [1]

The simultaneous kind was foreshadowed in
the famous ending of "Also Sprach Zarathustra," where the woodwind instruments sound
the chord of B major against the softly plucked
C of the strings; but we have to go to the
operas again to find it carried to its logical and
sometimes cruel extreme. There we find alien
triads marching uneasily together in double
harness; [2] dominant sevenths similarly
shackled; [3] and strange passages in which
the upper parts move naturally, but above a
dislocated bass. [4] Such procedures, which, it
must always be remembered, because of differences in tone quality between instruments
of different families, sound far less harsh in
the orchestra than on the piano, even if they
are no less queer musically, can theoretically be
carried to any extent. How far Strauss sometimes carries them, a single example must suffice to show.

[1] Vocal score, page 35.
[2] "Elektra," vocal score, page 21.
[3] *Ibid.* Page 23.
[4] *Ibid.* Page 20, the first line.

71

FIGURE IX.

Passage from "Elektra," vocal score, page 63.

Whether one "likes" such passages as this or not is of course a question of taste. But one thing at least is certain: it will not do to charge Strauss with mere musical anarchy in writing them — his work as a whole shows too keen a sense of the traditional harmonic values. That æsthetic insensibility, posing as "freedom from rules," "independence," "liberalism," and the like, to which in the minds of so many modern composers all keys are the same, is happily not one of his failings. That he has the keenest possible sense of the individual qualities of the different keys, and of the structural importance of their interrelationships, each one of his long series of symphonic poems has by its masterly design shown afresh. How remarkable, for example, is the antithesis of C, minor and major, and B, minor and major, which is the constructive principle of "Also Sprach Zarathustra!" How interesting is the choice of F major for the easy-going husband in the "Symphonia Domestica," and of the keener, more brilliant B major for the wife! And how this strong tonal sense not only guides the design as a whole, but suggests endless charming and imaginative details! At the end of the lullaby, in the same work, when the child has fallen asleep and the music has sunk to a tranquil G minor chord, this quietude is irradiated by a flash of B major and three notes of the wife-theme, — the loving tenderness of the waking and watching mother over the sleeping infant. Twice this happens, and each time the somnolent G minor returns. Thus does genius use tonality.

Being thus brought back to consider how Strauss uses all the elements of music, even

this subtlest one of contrasting tonalities, in
the interest of characterization, we may pon-
der with profit one final interpretation which
might seem over-ingenious had we not the
example of Mr. Klatte to spur our critical
imaginations. Why is it that we so seldom
hear the four tones of Till Eulenspiegel's main
theme on any other degrees of the scale than
A, F, B, C? Why is it that, in spite of the
constant movement from key to key of the
music, this theme is hardly ever carried also
into the new key?[1] Why does Strauss so insist on this A, F, B, C, not only when the
music is in F major, but when, as at Till's
anger, it is in D minor, when, as in the procession of the burghers, it is in A minor, and when,
just before the return of the main theme, it is
in C major? Why always A, F, B, C, whatever the key? Is it not because Till, half-
witted, perverse, self-imprisoned, is not subject
to social influences, and remains unplastically
himself, whatever his environment? To trans-
pose a theme into the key prevailing at the

---

[1] It *is* transposed into B flat in the episode wherein Till dons
the vestments of a priest.

moment is to make order — but Till represents disorder. . . . Such at least is the ingenious explanation of a woman who understands character as well as Strauss understands keys.

IV

All that we have been saying so far has concerned itself primarily with Strauss's powers of observation and characterization; we have noted how broad a field of human character he covers, and what varied artistic resources he brings to its depiction; we have seen how peculiarly fitted he is for this part of his work by his active temperament, with its accompanying intellectual alertness and freedom from self-consciousness. But we saw that the great dramatist needs not only observation but sympathy, in order that his work may be as moving as it is vivid; and in this power of emotion we may at first be inclined to consider Strauss deficient. There is undoubtedly a popular superstition which puts him among the intellectuals. The clean-cut efficiency of his personality, his businesslike habits, his mordant wit, both in words and in notes (was

there ever anything so witty as "Till Eulenspiegel"?), even questionably relevant details
like his exquisitely neat handwriting and his
well-groomed and not in the least long-haired
appearance,— all these create the impression
of a personality by no means *schwärmerisch*,
far removed indeed from the rapt dreamer
who is the school-girl's ideal composer.

There is perhaps a measure of truth in this
picture. Many of Strauss's most characteristic merits, as well as defects, may be traced
to his lack of the introspective tendency which
has been so fundamental in most of the other
great German musicians, from Bach to Wagner, and which is seen perhaps at its purest
and best in Schumann. Strauss is at the
other pole from Schumann — and music is
wide! Mr. Ernest Newman, in the ablest
studies of Strauss yet published in English,[1]
points to the internal evidence of this lack in
his earliest and therefore least sophisticated
compositions. "The general impression one

[1] "Richard Strauss," in the Living Masters of Music Series,
and "Richard Strauss and the Music of the Future," in "Musical
Studies."

gets from all these works," writes Mr. Newman, "is that of a head full to overflowing with music, a temperament that is energetic and forthright rather than warm . . . , and a general lack not only of young mannish sentimentality, but of sentiment. There is often a good deal of ardour in the writing, but it is the ardour of the intellect rather than of the emotions." And again: "Wherever the youthful Strauss has to sing rather than declaim, when he has to be emotional rather than intellectual, as in his slow movements, he almost invariably fails. . . . He feels it hard to squeeze a tear out of his unclouded young eyes, to make those taut, whip-cord young nerves of his quiver with emotion."[1]

Now, although Mr. Newman would not accept his own description of Strauss the youth as a fair account of the mature composer, although, indeed, he specifically insists, in a later passage, that Strauss's musical imagination lost, at adolescence, its "first metallic hardness" and "softened into something more purely emotional," yet his vivid phrases seem to

[1] "Richard Strauss," pages 30–32.

give us a picture of Strauss that is in essentials as true at fifty as it was at fifteen. "A temperament that is energetic and forthright rather than warm," "an ardour of the intellect rather than of the emotions" — these are surely still Straussian characteristics. And what is more they are characteristics that, whatever their dangers, have exerted a splendid influence in modern music. Schumann's was a noble introspection that no one who knows it can help loving; but in natures less pure the introspective habit of German romanticism has not always been so happy in its effects. An unhealthy degree of self-contemplation tends to substitute futile or morbid imaginings for the solid realities of life; the over-introspective artist cuts himself off from a large arc of experience and is prone to exaggerate the importance of the more intimate sentiments, and when, as in German romanticism, such a tendency is widespread, a whole school may become febrile and erotic. The vapors of such confirmed sentimentalism can best be dispersed by a ray of clear, cold intelligence, such as Shaw plays through contemporary literature and Strauss through contemporary music. "Cynicism," says Stevenson, " is the cold tub and bath towel of the emotions, and absolutely necessary to life in cases of advanced sensibility." Strauss has administered this tonic shock to us, immersed as we were in the languors of the Wagnerian boudoir. He has rooted us out of our agreeable reveries, sent us packing outdoors, and made us gasp with the stinging impacts of crude existence and the tingling lungfuls of fresh air. Is it not worth while, for this vigorous life, to sacrifice a few subtle nuances of feeling?

If then we so emphasize his possession of the active rather than the contemplative temperament, it is not to blame him for not being a Schumann, but to render as precise as possible in our own minds the notion of what it is to be a Strauss. If there is a point where blame or regret must mingle with our appreciation, it will be likely to come not at the preliminary determination of what his temperament is, but at the further discovery of certain extremes to which he has allowed his interest in externals to carry him, especially in his later work. And here we must try to set right a misconception with which Mr. Newman leaves the student of his essay on "Program Music."[1]

V

Mr. Newman, wishing to draw a reasoned distinction between self-sufficing, or "pure," or "abstract" music — that is, music that makes its appeal directly and without the aid of any verbal tag — and "poetic" music, or, more specifically, music with a definite program or title, adopts, seemingly without criticism, the popular notion that the first is less "emotional" than the second, and supports it by piling up epithets which beg the very question he is supposed to be examining. It is easy to "damn a dog by giving him a bad name," and it is easy to make music without program seem a dry and academic affair by calling it "abstract note-spinning," "mathematical music," "mere formal harmony," "embroidery," "juggling," "the arousing of pleasure in beautiful forms" — much too easy for a man of Mr. Newman's penetration and fair-

[1] In "Musical Studies."

mindedness. One expects this kind of thing from inexperienced youths whose enthusiasm has been inflamed by the gorgeous color and the easily grasped "story" of such a work as, let us say, Tschaikowsky's "Romeo and Juliet," who have not had time to live themselves into accord with the profound emotional life of the great musical classics such as Bach's fugues and Beethoven's symphonies; but from Mr. Newman such superficialities, especially when they are associated, as these are, with many penetrating and true observations, and an argument in the main convincing, come as a surprise.

The central fallacy that vitiates Mr. Newman's conclusions lurks in his assumption that "specific reference to actual life" necessarily means greater emotion, and that the generality or "abstractness" of classic music is a symptom of emotional deficiency. "In the old symphony or sonata," says Mr. Newman, "a succession of notes, pleasing in itself but not having specific reference to actual life — not attempting, that is, to get at very close quarters with strong emotional or dramatic expression, but influencing and affecting us mainly by reason of its purely formal relations and by the purely physical pleasure inherent in it as sound — was stated, varied, worked out, and combined with other themes of the same order. . . ." And again : "The opening phrase of Beethoven's 8th Symphony refers to nothing at all external to itself; it is what Herbert Spencer has called the music of pure exhilaration; to appreciate it you have to think of nothing but itself; the pleasure lies primarily in the way the notes are put together." To this a footnote is appended : "There is emotion, of course, at the back of the notes; the reader will not take me to mean that the pleasure is merely physical, like a taste or an odour. But the emotive wave is relatively small and very vague; it neither comes directly from nor suggests any external existence." Once more, the assumption that degree of emotion is in a direct ratio with externality of suggestion.

But as a matter of fact is not the exact opposite the truth? Are we not most deeply moved when we are lifted clean out of the concrete and carried up to the universal of

which it is only an example? Is not the general
far more moving than the particular? Do we
not feel external details to be irrelevant and
even annoyingly intrusive when we are stirred
to the recognition of inward truths, of spiritual
realities? No doubt program music owes to
its reference to the particular story, the well-
known hero, the familiar book or picture, a
certain vividness, an immediateness of appeal
even to the unmusical, a rich fund of associations to draw upon; but even program music,
surely, tends in all its more powerful moments to penetrate below this comparatively
superficial layer of external facts to the pro-
founder (and of course vaguer) emotional
strata of which they are, so to speak, the out-
croppings. It is odd how little difference there
is between program music and music, without
the tag, in their more inspired moments; in
all symphonic poems it is the symphonic rather
than the poetic element that is chiefly responsible for the effect produced; and indeed, in-
creasingly realistic as Strauss has become in
his later works, even here the memorable moments are those of emotional fulfilment and

realization, in which we tacitly agree to let the program go hang. Far from the "emotive wave" being proportional to the suggestion of "external existence," then, one would say that it was rather proportional to the realization of universal spiritual truth, and that in systematically confronting us with ever more and more crassly external existences Strauss has in his later works followed a practice as questionable as the theory which supports it, and levied an ever greater tax of boredom on our joy in the finer moments of his art.

Even in "Tod und Verklärung," which remains to this day, in the words of M. Romain Rolland,[1] "one of the most moving works of Strauss, and that which is constructed with the noblest unity," the repulsively realistic details with which the gasping for breath of the dying man is pictured consort but incongruously with the tender beauty of the "childhood" passages and the broad grandeur of the "transfiguration." The love of crass realism thus early revealed has grown apace, by even steps, unfortunately, with the extraordinary

1 "Musiciens d'aujourd'hui," page 123.

powers upon which it is parasitic. In the works conceived partially in a spirit of comedy, to be sure, such as "Till Eulenspiegel" and "Don Quixote," it finds a whimsical, witty expression for itself which not only seldom strikes a false note, but is often exceedingly amusing. Till's charge among the market-women's pots and pans, the bleating of the sheep in "Don Quixote," even perhaps the baby's squalling in the "Symphonia Domestica," are clever bits of side play, like the "business" of an irrepressible comedian, which are not out of key with the main substance of the music. But even here these realistic touches are exuberances, and inessential; the essential thing in "Till," for example, is the spirit of mischief and destruction that existed in the human heart for centuries before the rascal Eulenspiegel was born, and that respond in us to his pranks; and this essence Strauss expresses in the purely musical parts of his work, and by means identical in kind with those employed in a Beethoven scherzo.

And if realistic detail is in such instances subordinate to musical expression it may in the treatment of more serious subjects become positively inimical to it. Do we really care very much about supermen and "convalescents" and the rival claims of Christianity and neo-paganism when we are listening to "Also Sprach Zarathustra"? Does not that everlasting C-G-C, with its insistence on an esoteric meaning that we never knew or have forgotten, pester us unnecessarily? What we remember in "Zarathustra" is much more likely to be the poignant passion of the "Grablied," or the beautiful broad melody of the violins, in B major, near the end, which bears no label at all save the tempo mark "Langsam." Similarly, in the "Symphonia Domestica" the family squabbles, growling father giving the replique to bawling infant, leave us skeptically detached or mildly amused. It is the musical charm of the "easy-going" parts in F major, the cradle song, above all the largely conceived slow movement with its wonderful development of the husband's "dreamy" theme, that really stir us. As for "Ein Heldenleben," what an unmitigated bore are those everlasting Adversaries!

Thus in the later works Strauss's shortcomings on the subjective side, his native tendency to concern himself more with concrete appearances than with essential emotional truths, seem exaggerated to such a degree as seriously to disturb the balance of his art. As he has interested himself more and more in externals he has not entirely evaded the danger of exalting the "program" at the expense of the "music," and his work, for all its extraordinary brilliance, its virtuosity, its power, has become over-emphatic, ill-balanced, hard in finish and theatrical in emphasis. It is ultimately a spiritual defect that compels us to withhold our full admiration from "Ein Heldenleben" or the "Domestica." We admit their titanic power, their marvelous nervous vitality; their technical temerities grow for the most part acceptable with familiarity; it is their emotional unreality that disappoints us. This charge of unreality, made against realism, may surprise us, may seem to savor of paradox; but it is inevitable. For music, as we have been told *ad nauseam*, but as we must never be allowed to forget, exists to express feeling; the only truth essential to it is truth to emotion; and therefore realism, looking as it does away from inward emotion to external fact, ever tends toward musical unreality.

How shall we account for this progressive externalizing of Strauss's musical interest? Is it all temperament? Has environment had anything to do with it? Do those high-sounding but dubious things "modern German materialism" and its accompanying æsthetic "decadence" bear in any way upon the matter? These are questions too large for a humble annalist of music to answer. M. Romain Rolland, however, in his essay on French and German Music in "Musiciens d'aujourd'hui," has one suggestion too relevant to be neglected here. "German music," says M. Rolland, "loses from day to day its intimateness: there is some of it still in Wolf, thanks to the exceptional misfortunes of his life; there is very little of it in Mahler, despite his efforts to concentrate himself upon himself; there is hardly any of it in Strauss, although he is the most interesting of the three. They no longer have any depth. I have said that I attribute

this fact to the detestable influence of the
theatre, to which almost all these artists are
attached, as Kapellmeisters, directors of opera,
etc. They owe to it the often melodramatic
or at least external character of their music —
music on parade, thinking constantly of effect."

One hesitates to accept so damning a charge
as this against any artist, especially against a
musical artist, who above all others should
render sincere account of what is in his own
heart rather than "give the public what it
wants." Yet there is only too much in the
later Strauss that it explains. How else shall
we account for the exaggerated emphasis, the
over-elaboration of contrasts that seem at
times almost mechanical, and that suggest
shrewd calculation of the crowd psychology
rather than free development of the musical
thought? What else explains so well the sensational elements so incredibly childish in an
art so mature as Strauss's: the ever-increasing
noisiness, the introduction of wind-machines,
thunder-machines, and heaven knows what
diabolic engines; the appetite for novelty for
novelty's sake? And is there not a reflection

of the "saponaceous influences of opera," as Sir Hubert Parry so well calls them, in the cloying over-sweetness, the sensuous luxury, of those peculiar passages, like the oboe solo in "Don Juan," the love music in "Ein Heldenleben," which form such conventional spots in the otherwise vital tissue of the music? Surely the opera house, and not the concert hall, is the place where such sybaritisms naturally breed.

For one reason and another, then — temperament, environment, the enervation of the operatic atmosphere with its constant quest of "effect" — the fresh and vital elements in Strauss's art have not entirely escaped contamination by more stale, conventional, and specious ones. Particularly has he failed of his highest achievement when desire for immediate appeal, the bias of an over-active mind, or the fallacies of a one-sided æsthetic have led him too far from the subjective emotion which is truly the soul of music. Yet when all subtractions are made he must remain one of the great creative musicians of his day. His surprising vigor and trenchancy of mind, his wit, his sense of comedy (in the Meredithian use of the word), his unerring eye for character, and, at his best, his sympathetic interpretation of life and his broad grasp of its significance as a whole, combine to produce a unique personality. Some of the eloquence we find in the more pompous parts of "Zarathustra" or "Ein Heldenleben" posterity will probably dismiss as bombast; but posterity will be stupid indeed if it does not prize "Till Eulenspiegel" and "Don Quixote" as master expressions of the spirit of comedy in music. "Till Eulenspiegel" particularly is a well-nigh perfect blending of the three qualities of the master dramatist we began by discussing. It combines the observation of a Swift with the sympathetic imagination of a Thackeray. Beneath its turbulent surface of fun is a deep sense of pathos, of the fragmentariness and fleetingness of Till, for all his pranks; so that to the sensitive it may easily bring tears as well as smiles. Above all, it has that largeness of vision, rarest of artistic qualities, which not only penetrates from appearance to feeling, but grasps feeling in all its relations, presents a unified picture of life, and purges the emotions as the Greek tragedy aimed to do. All is suffused in beauty. The prologue: "Once upon a time there was a man," and the epilogue: "Thus it happened to Till Eulenspiegel," make a complete cycle of the work, and remove its expression to a philosophic or poetic plane high above mere crude realism. There are doubtless more impressive single passages in later works, but it may be doubted if anything Strauss has ever written is more perfect or more tender than this wittiest of pieces, in which the wit is yet forgotten in the beauty.

III
SIR EDWARD ELGAR

Edward Elgar.

III

SIR EDWARD ELGAR

HE most inspiring chapters of musical history are those that tell of the struggles of great men, spurred by the desire for free, sincere, and personal speech, to wrest the musical language out of the triteness long conventional usage has given it; to make it say something new; to add, so to speak, to the impersonal organ chord it sounds an overtone of their particular human voices. This is what stirs us when we think of Beethoven, after he had written two symphonies in the style of Haydn and Mozart, finding himself at the opening of "a new road," leading he knew not whither, but irresistibly summoning him; of Gluck, at fifty, protesting against the hollowness of the Italian operas he had been writing up to that time; of Franck, still older, finding at last the secret of that vague, groping, mystical harmonic style he made so peculiarly his own. Men dread liberty, says Bernard Shaw, because of the bewildering responsibility it imposes and the uncommon alertness it demands; no wonder that they acclaim as truly great only those artists who fully accept this responsibility and successfully display this alertness. And it may be suggested that the more conventional, and therefore paralyzing to personal initiative, the style from which the artist takes his departure, the more alertness does he require, and the more credit does he deserve if he arrives at freedom. If this be true, Sir Edward Elgar, who, starting at English oratorio, has arrived at the cosmopolitan yet completely individual musical speech of the first Symphony, the Variations, and parts of "The Dream of Gerontius," is surely one of the great men of our time.

For nothing, not even stark crudity, is so unfavorable to artistic life as the domination by a conventional formalism like that of the Handel-Mendelssohn school from which Elgar had to start. It may take a great artist like Dvořák or Verdi to build an art on the naïvetés of Bohemian folk-song or the banalities of Italian opera; but to free an art from the tyranny of drowsy custom, as Elgar has done, requires not only a great artist, but something of a revolutionary.

Elgar is English in character, but cosmopolitan in sympathies, style, and workmanship. In other words, while retaining the personal and racial quality natural to all sincere art, he has been magnanimous, intelligent, and unconventional enough to break through the charmed circle of insularity which has kept so many English composers from vital contact with the world. Such insularity cannot but be fatal to art. It is bad enough when it confines the artist to narrow native models. It is even worse when, ignoring native music of the finest quality, such as that of Purcell, it follows blindly, through timidity or inertia, traditions imported by foreigners of inferior grade. Generations of English musicians have stultified themselves in imitating Handel's burly ponderousness and Mendelssohn's somewhat vapid elegance. They have turned a deaf ear, not only to the greater contemporaries of these idols — to Bach and to Schumann — but also to the more modern thought of Wagner, Franck, Tschaikowsky, and Brahms. They have been correct and respectable in an art which lives only through intense personal emotion. They have narrowed their sympathies. They have been national in an age of dawning internationalism.

Elgar, on the contrary, together with a few others whose work deserves to be better known than it is, has had the courage to aspire to a cosmopolitan breadth of style. He has made up for the lack of what are called "educational advantages" by something far more valuable — an insatiable intellectual curiosity. Self-taught except for a few violin lessons in youth, he has been all his life a tireless listener, observer, and student. When he was a boy, having no text-books on musical form, he wrote a whole symphony in imitation of Mozart's in G minor, "following the leader" with admirable and fruitful docility. As a youth he would play violin, at the last desk oftentimes, in any orchestra to which he could gain admission, for the sake of the experience; and between rehearsals would laboriously collate the instrumental parts to find out why a certain passage sounded well or ill. He would travel two hundred and fifty miles to London, from his home in Worcester, to hear a Crystal Palace Saturday concert, returning late at night. Knowing well that any potent individuality like his own grows by what it assimilates, he has had none of the small man's fear of injuring by the study of others his "individuality." The internal evidence of his works shows that there are few modern scores he has left unpondered; yet no living composer has a more unmistakably personal style than his.

His intellectual activity has by no means confined itself to music. He has always been an omnivorous reader. And while much of this reading naturally proceeded in desultory fashion, for the sake of relaxation, and took him sometimes as far afield as Froissart, the fourteenth-century French chronicler, as suggested by his early overture of that name, he has never lost the power of concentration, and can study a book to as good purpose as a score. His analytic notes to his symphonic study

"Falstaff" (1913) reveal a surprisingly detailed knowledge both of Shakespeare and of Shakespeare's commentators. Science also interests him, and for some years his hobby was scientific kite-flying. He is of the nervously irritable temperament so often coupled with mental alertness, walks about restlessly while conversing, and detests all routine work like teaching. "To teach the right pupil was a pleasure," he once said, "but teaching in general was to me like turning a grindstone with a dislocated shoulder." In 1889 he married, gave up most of his teaching, and moved to London. Since then he has lived partly among his native Malvern Hills, partly near London, but has devoted himself almost entirely to composing and conducting.

Elgar's whole life has thus been a gradual and progressive self-emancipation from the limitations of inherited style, an escape from habit to initiative, from formality to eloquence, from insularity to cosmopolitanism. Nor has this progress been the less inspiring in that it has been spasmodic, subject to interruptions, and never complete. In that respect it shares

the lovable imperfection of all things human.
It has been instinctive rather than reasoned,
has proceeded largely by trial and error, and
has counted among its experiments almost as
many failures as successes. There are commonplace pages in almost everything Elgar
has written, unless it be the "Enigma" Variations. But the important point is that however much, in moments of technical inattention
or emotional indifference, he may fall back into
the formulæ of his school, he has at his best
left them far behind, and made himself the
peer of his greatest continental contemporaries
in wealth and variety of expression — of such
men as Strauss in Germany and d'Indy in
France.

What are these never-quite-ejected formulæ,
lurking in Elgar's brain, ever ready to guide
his pen when for a moment he forgets to think
and feel? If we look at the opening chorus
of "The Black Knight," written in 1893, and
numbered opus 25, we shall get a working notion
of them (Figure X, page 102).

How this passage calls up the atmosphere
of the typical English choral festival: the

FIGURE X.

Opening chorus from "The Black Knight."

Allegro maestoso

unwieldy masses of singers, the scarcely less unwieldy orchestra or organ, the ponderous movement of the music, half majestic, half tottering, as of a drunken elephant, the well-meaning ineptitude of the expression, highly charged with good nature but innocent of nuance! There is the solid diatonic harmony, conscientiously divided between the four equally industrious parts. There is the thin disguising of the tendency of this hymn-tune type of harmony to sit down, so to speak, on the accent of each measure, by a few conventional suspensions. There is the attempt to give the essentially stagnant melody a specious air of busyness by putting in a triplet here and a dot or short rest there. And there is the sing-song phraseology by which a phrase of four measures follows a phrase of four measures as the night the day. In short, there is the perfectly respectable production of music by the yard, on the most approved pattern, undistorted by a breath of personal feeling or imagination.

How far Elgar, whenever his imagination is stirred, can get away from this conventional vacuity, even without departing materially from its general idiom, may as well be shown at once, for the sake of the illuminating contrast, by the quotation of a bit of genuine Elgar — the "Nimrod" in the "Enigma" Variations, opus 36 (1899).

This touching tribute to a friend of the composer, Mr. A. J. Jaeger (the English equivalent of whose name, hunter, suggested the title), has all the serious thoughtfulness, the tenderness coupled with aspiration, the noble plainness, that belong to Elgar at his best. And

FIGURE XI.

"Nimrod," from the "Enigma Variations."

it is a striking fact that the originality of the
passage (for no one but Elgar could have
written it) is due to subtle, almost unanalyzable
qualities in the mode of composition rather
than to any unusual features of style. The
harmonic style, indeed, is quite the same simple
diatonic one as that of "The Black Knight"
chorus, showing that, in music as in literature,
noble poetry can be made from the same materials as doggerel. There is the same pre-
dominance of simple triads and seventh chords,
especially the more rugged sevenths, for which
Elgar has a noticeable fondness; the same

frequent use of suspensions, though here it is dictated by emotion rather than by custom; the same restless motion of the bass, one of the hall-marks of Elgar's style. The melody, however, shows a tendency to large leaps, often of a seventh, in alternating directions, giving its line a sharply serrated profile. This, it may be noted, is also one of the outstanding features of his more personal thought. But above all should be observed the rhythmic flexibility that here takes the place of sing-song — the free sweep of the line, scorning to rest on the accents, soaring through its long continuous flight like a bird in a favoring gale.

We have here, then, the vein of expression at once plain, serious, and noble, which makes Elgar at his best both English and universal. It recurs frequently throughout the whole body of his work: in the "Go forth" chorus in "Gerontius," so finely used in the prelude; in the theme of the Variations; in the fundamental theme of the first Symphony, which dominates the entire work and in which Elgar reaches perhaps his most exalted utterance; in the themes of the slow movement of the same symphony; and in another way in the Prince Hal theme of "Falstaff." Some may feel that this is the essential Elgar. Yet there is also in this quiet Englishman a passionate mysticism, a sense of subtle spiritual experience, which has urged him to develop progressively quite another mode of musical speech. On this side he is related to Wagner and to César Franck. Like them he has realized that there is a whole range of feeling, inaccessible to the diatonic system of harmony, that can be suggested by harmony based on the chromatic scale, and even more vividly and subtly by a harmonic system that opens up a path between all the keys, that makes them all available together — by what we may call, in short, "polytonal" harmony. This polytonal harmonic system is common to "Tristan und Isolde," to Franck's "Les Béatitudes," to much of Chopin, and to many parts of "The Dream of Gerontius," however much they may differ in other respects.

Elgar began early to experiment in this direction. Even in "The Black Knight," for example, at the word "rock" in the lines

When he rode into the lists
The castle 'gan to rock,

we have the following progression, equally striking from the musical and the dramatic point of view:

FIGURE XII.

From "The Black Knight."

Allegro molto e con fuoco

This is what Mr. Carl W. Grimm has well named a "modulating sequence"; that is, each unit group of harmony (in this case a measure in length) is the sequential repetition of the preceding, yet the chromatic texture is so managed that each begins in a new key; the total effect is thus much more novel and exciting than is that of the traditional mono-tonal sequence. Yet, as Mr. Stillman-Kelley has pointed out in a closely reasoned essay,[1]

[1] "Recent Developments in Musical Theory," by Edgar Stillman-Kelley. The Musical Courier, July 1 and 8, 1908.

however ingenious may be the arrangement of the modulating sequence on the harmonic side, it is liable to the same fault that besets the monotonal sequence — that is, rhythmic monotony. Once we have the pattern, we know what to expect; and if the composer gives us exactly what we expect the effect is too obvious, and we are bored. It is precisely by his avoidance of this literal repetition, says Mr. Kelley, that Wagner, in such a modulating sequence as that of the Pilgrims' Chorus, maintains both the rhythmic and the harmonic vitality of the music.

Judged by the standard thus suggested, the sequence on the word "rock" is seen to be too literally carried out. The pattern is applied with the mechanical regularity of a stencil, necessarily with an equally mechanical result. It must be said in the interest of just criticism that Elgar frequently falls into this fault. Even Gerontius' cry of despair, so magnificently developed by the orchestra, contains less of subtle variety than is given to that curiously similar cry of Amfortas in "Parsifal" by the "inversion" of the parts, while the priest's adjuration to his departing soul[1] and the chorus afterward based on it, become irritatingly monotonous through the literal repetition of a pattern admirable in itself. At the beginning of the Development in the first movement of the second Symphony there is a passage illustrating the same fault. The tonal and harmonic coloring here are singularly impressive, and quite original; as Mr. Ernest Newman remarks in his analysis:[2] "A new and less sunny cast has come over the old themes. . . . The harmonies have grown more mysterious; the scoring is more veiled; the dynamics are all on a lower scale." Everything favors, in fact, a most impressive effect except the structure; but that, through its over-literal application of the modulating sequence, almost jeopardizes the whole.

Fortunately, however, happier applications of this harmonically so fruitful device are not far to seek in Elgar's scores, especially the later ones. The following theme from "The Apostles," appropriately marked "mistico," is

[1] Vocal score, page 39.
[2] Musical Times, London, May 1, 1911.

a fine example of the kind of mysticism that is not unmindful of the needs of the body and of the intelligence as well as of the soul.

FIGURE XIII.

In the Mountain, — Night.   From "The Apostles."

The principle is still that of the modulating sequence, but the application is here not mechanical but freely imaginative. Two of the one-measure units are in each phrase balanced by a unit twice as long, so that the rhythm is as a whole far more organic than in our earlier examples of sequences. Furthermore the purely harmonic treatment makes use of unforeseeable relations, so that the effect of stere-

otype is successfully evaded. Finally, here is
a theme from the second symphony in which
the sequential principle is still further veiled,
so far as harmony is concerned. The harmonic progressions seem here to "shoot," so
to speak, with complete spontaneity; we cannot anticipate whither the next move will take
us, and we get constantly to interesting new
places; yet the unity of the whole, beginning
and ending in E-flat [1], prevents any sense of
aimless wandering.

FIGURE XIV.

Theme from Symphony No. 2.

[1] Is not Mr. Newman mistaken in stating that this theme begins in G major?

The alert student will probably still feel, nevertheless, perhaps without being able to account in any way for his impression, that even in these last excerpts there is an unsatisfactory element, a something that keeps them on a lower level of art, for all their opaline color, than that of the forthright and transparent "Nimrod." This something, perhaps on the whole Elgar's most ineradicable fault, is rhythmical "short breath." He gets away from it, to be sure, in all his finest pages; but except when his imagination is deeply stirred his melodic line shows the dangerous tendency to fall into short segments, a measure or two in length, into a configuration of scallops, so to speak, rather than wide sweeps, exemplified in the three last illustrations. Instead of flying, it hops. Examples will be found right through his works, from the second theme of the early overture "Froissart" to that of the first movement of the Violin Concerto, opus 61.

FIGURE XV.

Second theme from "Froissart."

Second theme of first movement of Violin Concerto.

This kind of sing-songiness is as fatal to noble rhythm in music as it is in poetry — in much of Longfellow, for example; and the frequency with which Elgar relapses into it suggests that he has some of the same fatal facility, the tendency to talk without thinking, which so often kept the American poet below his best. The parallel might be carried out, if it were worth while, in some detail. Both men wrote too much, and both are "popular" in the bad sense as well as the good. The "Pomp and Circumstance" Marches are saved, despite the frequent triteness of their melody, by their buoyant high spirits; but of the vapid and sentimental "Salut d'Amour," which has sold in the thousands and been arranged for all possible combinations of instruments, including two mandolins and a guitar, the less said the better. Yet it is noteworthy that the very tendency to an over-obvious, monotonous rhythmic scheme which works for the popularity of a small piece with the thoughtless and trivial-minded, works against it in the case of a larger composition which appeals to the musically serious, and wins its way gradually at best. Thus Elgar's second symphony, which suffers much more from this besetting fault than the first, has been less popular for that very reason. Statistics are significant in such cases. The second symphony was played twenty-seven times before it was three years old, a considerable number for so serious a work [1]; but the first, called by Nikisch "Brahms's Fifth," a compliment which could be paid to few other modern symphonies without absurdity, achieved the almost incredible record of eighty-two performances in its first year, in such widely scattered places as London, Vienna, Berlin, Leipsic, Bonn, St. Petersburg, Buda Pest, Toronto, Sydney, and the United States.[2]

Of course it is not intended to account for the wide favor accorded this symphony by

[1] Musical Times, January, 1914.
[2] Musical Times, January, 1909.

adducing so technical a matter, from one point of view, as its comparative freedom from a rhythmic weakness to which its composer is unfortunately peculiarly subject. What is meant is simply that sing-song balance of short phrases is often a symptom of superficial feeling, and that, *per contra*, elastic, vigorous, and imaginative rhythms are a constant result, and therefore a reliable evidence, of the emotional ardor that makes a piece of music live. The A-flat Symphony is a work intensely felt by the composer, a work that, coming from his heart, finds its way to the hearts of others. And in this respect, in its emotional sincerity, earnestness, and subjectivity, it differs from his other works more in degree than in kind. For in everything Elgar writes there is the preoccupation with inner feeling which we find in such a composer as Schumann, but from which most of our contemporaries have turned away. Elgar is an introspective musician, not an externally observant tone-painter like Strauss. It is noteworthy how completely his treatment of death, for example, in "The Dream of Gerontius," differs from that of Strauss in

"Tod und Verklärung." By no means accidental is it, but highly significant of the opposed attitudes of the two artists, that while Strauss emphasizes the external picture — the panting breath, the choking cries — Elgar penetrates to the inward emotional state. He has written surprisingly little program music. Aside from a few realistic touches scattered through the choral works, and the delicate little vignette of the friend at sea in the "Enigma" Variations, there is only "Falstaff" — and that deals more with character than with picture. In this respect Elgar deserves well of his contemporaries for standing against a popular but dangerous tendency to externalize the most inward of the arts, and for showing that even in the twentieth century the spiritual drama set forth in a work of pure music, like his first symphony, can be as thrilling as those that have made immortal Beethoven's later quartets and sonatas.

That this attitude indicates a preference rather than a limitation is proved by the felicity of the external characterization in passages scattered all through the choral works, as for instance the setting of the line "The castle 'gan to rock," cited above, from the "Black Knight," the music of the devils in "Gerontius," or the scene in "The Apostles" where Peter walks upon the water, and even more strikingly in "Falstaff," the composer's single contribution to program music. Here he frankly takes the Straussian attitude, and skilfully uses the Straussian methods. Leading themes, as he tells us in his analysis,[1] depict the fat knight, one "in a green old age, mellow, frank, gay, easy, corpulent, loose, unprincipled,

FIGURE XVI.

Three of the "Falstaff" themes.

[1] Musical Times, September, 1913.

117

and luxurious" (*a*); another "cajoling and persuasive" (*b*); and a third in his mood of "boastfulness and colossal mendacity" (*c*).

These portraits evidently belong to the same gallery as Strauss's Don Quixote, Sancho Panza (*cf.* the first quotation), Till Eulenspiegel, and others; they are sketched in the same suggestive and telling lines; in the third there is even the same touch of caricature. The picture of Eastcheap, too, where, "among ostlers and carriers, and drawers, and merchants, and pilgrims and loud robustious women, Falstaff has freedom and frolic," has something of the German composer's brilliant externality. It should, as Elgar says in his notes, and it does, "chatter, blaze, glitter, and coruscate." Yet, vivid as all this is, even here from time to time, notably in the two "interludes," the composer characteristically withdraws from the turbulent outer world he has conjured up, to brood upon its spiritual meaning; and it is noteworthy that after stating in his analysis that "some lines quoted from the plays are occasionally placed under the themes to indicate the feeling to be conveyed by the music," he immediately adds, "but it is not intended that the meaning of the music, often varied and intensified, shall be narrowed to a corollary of these quotations only." This intensification arises, of course, through the universalizing of all the particulars by the power of music to express pure emotion.

The same instinctive leaning to introspection is curiously shown in the Enigma Variations.[1] "I have in the Variations," writes Elgar in a private letter, "sketched portraits of my friends — a new idea, I think — that is, in each variation I have looked at the theme through the personality (as it were) of another Johnny." The idea was not indeed quite new, however originally applied, as Schumann had already sketched a number of his friends in the "Carnaval." But what is of much greater import is that Schumann and Elgar, both introspective temperaments, go about this business of portrait painting in the same characteristic way — not by recording the external aspects of these "other Johnnies," but by

[1] Arranged for piano by the composer. Novello, Ewer, and Company, London.

sympathetically putting themselves at their points of view and becoming, so to speak, the spokesmen of their souls. The tender intimateness of Elgar's interpretations is their supreme charm. Whatever the character portrayed, whether the tender grace of C. A. E. (Lady Elgar), the caprice of H. D. S-P., the virile energy of W. M. B., the gossamer delicacy of Dorabelle, or the nobility of "Nimrod," we feel in each case that we have for the moment really got inside the personality, and looked at the world along that unique perspective. Even in the indescribably lovely Romanza, Variation XIII, calling up the thought of a friend at sea, though programistic devices are used, the spirit looks away from externalities. Violas in a quietly undulating rhythm suggest the ocean expanse; an almost inaudible tremolo of the drum gives us the soft throb of the engines; a quotation from Mendelssohn's "Calm Sea and Prosperous Voyage," in the dreamy tones of the clarinet, completes the story. Yet "story" it is not — and there is the subtlety of it. Dim sea and dream-like steamer are only accessories after all. The thought of the distant friend, the human soul there, is what gently disengages itself as the essence of the music.

In his two symphonies the composer gives us even less encouragement to search for detailed programs. It is true that the second bears the motto from Shelley:

> Rarely, rarely, comest thou,
> Spirit of Delight.

But it will be observed, first, that these lines contain no pictorial images which would prevent their application to the most purely emotional music — a symphony of Beethoven, for example; and second, that even their emotional bearing is somewhat ambiguous, as we are left in doubt whether it is the Spirit of Delight itself, or the rareness of its visitations, that we are asked to consider. Mr. Ernest Newman thinks the former, and finds in the symphony the "jocundity and sweetness" which characterize English music from the earliest times. We read in the Musical Times,[1] however, that there is "some disagreement . . . with the composer's own opinion

[1] July, 1911.

that it is on a totally different psychological plane from that of the first symphony, and represents a more serene mood," although the writer adds that "it is unquestionable that the themes, even in the slow movement, speak of a lighter heart and more tranquil emotions." If there is thus room for doubt even as to the emotional content of the work, no attempt to read into it a "story" is likely to be successful. Even Mr. Newman, programist *à outrance*, is forced in this case to the admission that "though practically every musical work of any emotional value must start from this basis [of the composer's life-experience],[1] the connection of it with the external world or with the symbols of the literary and plastic arts may range through many degrees of vagueness or precision, according to the psychological build of the composer."

Coming now at last to Elgar's masterpiece,

[1] This premise, which Mr. Newman expands as if it bore directly on the problem of program music, though true to the verge of truism, hardly helps us to solve that problem. The question, it may be said once again, concerns not the composer's stimulus, but his method; whether, that is, he works through the suggestion of external objects or of inner emotional states.

the Symphony [1] in A-flat, No. 1, opus 55, first performed under Dr. Hans Richter at Manchester and at London in December, 1908, we find Elgar's method at its purest — the preoccupation with spiritual states and experiences is complete. It is true that this may be the symphony upon which he was reported nine years earlier to be at work, and which was to bear the title "Gordon." If this is the case it shows only that he was moved to musical expression by the heroism of the great Englishman, as Beethoven was by that of Napoleon before it transpired that he was a tyrant. The A-flat Symphony is not for that reason any more program music than Beethoven's "Eroica." The two are indeed similar in being throughout profound searchings of the human spirit, highly dramatic in the vividness of their introspection, but never realistic. They penetrate to a level far deeper than that of action; they deal with the emotional springs of action; we may even say that each suggests a philosophy, since the philosophies, too, are

[1] Arrangement for piano by S. Karg-Elert. Novello, Ewer, and Company.

born of those deep inarticulate emotional attitudes toward life which only music can voice in their purity.

This fundamental attitude is in the A-flat Symphony far more mature and chastened than that of the ebulliently youthful "Eroica." If we wished to find its analogue in Beethoven (and it is a high compliment to Elgar to say that there are few other places we could find it) we should have to go rather to the Ninth Symphony and to the later sonatas and quartets. It is in essence the attitude of religious resignation, and has as its constituents the primary opposition between the ideal and reality, the disappointment, softening, and impersonalizing of the soul by experience, the reciprocal activity of the soul winning its values out of experience, and the final reconciliation between them. Of course it is not meant that these ideas are intellectually formulated in the music. It is simply that the music expresses the emotional states that accompany such universal human experiences, and thus suggests and at the same time by its beauty transfigures them.

The noble melody in A-flat major with which

the symphony starts, recurring in the finale, and indeed the nucleus of the whole work, suggests aspiration, resolute will, the quest of the Ideal. Everything about it, — its steady movement, its simple, strong harmonic basis, its finely flexible rhythm, notably free from the short breath of the composer's less exalted moments, even its rich and yet quiet tonality of A-flat major, raises it into a rarefied atmosphere of its own, above the turmoil of everyday life. With the theme in D minor marked Allegro appassionato, on the contrary, we are brought rudely down to earth, with all its confusion, its chaos, its meaningless accidents (note the constant feverish motion of the bass, the phantasmagoric nightmare harmonies at index letter 7, the increasing restlessness of the whole passage). Presently more poignant or tender phrases (10 and 11) suggest the longing of the spirit for the sweet reasonableness of the lost ideal world, and at 12, in the "second theme" in F major, we do get for a moment a breathing interval of peace. The beautiful, tender phrase, as of divine pity, beginning in the fourth measure of 11 and ushering in this theme, should be especially noticed for its deep expressiveness and its complete originality. This "phrase of pity," as we shall see, is destined to play an important part in the structure of the movement. Soon earlier fragments return, reintroducing the restless mood, the intensity of the feeling steadily grows, and at 17 we have a magnificent climax in which the "phrase of pity," much slower and more emphatic than before, suggests the first crisis of the struggle.

With the return of the theme of the ideal, now in C major (18) and in tentative accents, begins the long and complex development of the themes. We need not go into detail here, further than to remark that the strange, devious new theme at 24 seems almost to have some concrete "meaning," undisclosed by the composer, and introduces the most baffling element we find anywhere in the symphony. The development proceeds much upon it. At 32 begins the recapitulation of themes of the orthodox sonata-form, treated freely and with many interesting modifications. The climax recurs at 44, now impressively amplified. Even finer is

the gradual but irresistible return of the fundamental theme, the "Ideal," and its triumphant
statement through 49, 50, and 51. The sinister,
groping theme returns, however, seeming to
darken the atmosphere as when clouds come
over the sun. The "Ideal" theme is heard
in faltering, uncertain accents, and reaches,
just before 55, a timid cadence on the tone C.
Now comes one of the most exquisite things,
not only in this symphony, but in modern
music. While the clarinet holds this C, reached
in the original key of A-flat major, the muted
strings, high and tenuous, in the remote key of
A minor, like voices from another world, gently
breathe the "phrase of pity." It is magical.
With fine dignity of pace they reach the tone
C, whereupon we are again quietly but con-
clusively brought back to A-flat, and with a
single plucked bass note the chord of the clarinets sinks to silence (Figure XVII, page 128).

The two middle movements of the symphony,
Allegro molto (the scherzo) and Adagio, are
played without intervening pause and conceived together. From the point of view both
of form and of content their treatment is

FIGURE XVII.

End of first movement, First Symphony.

of exceeding interest. Structurally they are
an inset between the first movement and the
finale, contrasting sharply with them in key
as well as in melodic material, embodying as
they do the "sharp" keys (F-sharp minor and
D major) in opposition to the A-flat major and
D minor of the others. After this inset has
been completed, the earlier themes and keys
return in the finale and round out the cycle
projected by the first movement. Thus the
symphony as a whole consists of two interlocking systems — a scheme of structure which

gives it both variety and unity in the highest degree.

The scherzo begins with a racing, eagerly hurrying theme, staccato, in the violins, in the fastest possible tempo. Together with a more vigorous, barbarically insistent tune to which it presently (59) gives place, it seems a musical expression of the forward-looking, all-conquering spirit of youth. These themes are separately elaborated, are displaced for a while by a quieter Trio, and finally return with renewed vigor, and at last in combination (75). And now, as coda, comes one of the most remarkable passages of the Symphony. The racing theme returns (82), but now pianissimo, mysterious, shorn of its pristine exuberance. It hesitates, halts, seems to lose faith in itself. It reappears in the more sombre key of F minor, instead of F-sharp minor, and with abated pace (84). A little later it sobers to a still quieter movement, in eighth notes (86), then (87) to quarter notes, and at last (90) the clarinets give it out in a movement eight times slower than the original headlong dash. Indeed, the rhythm seems about to fail entirely when, with a change of key to D major, and of time to Adagio, we hear the identical notes of the original theme, sung now with broad deliberation by the violins, completely transfigured in meaning.

Thus begins the slow movement with the coming of maturity, the taming of the blood, the sadness of self-acquaintance no longer to be postponed. The excitement of unlimited possibilities gives place to the sober recognition of limitations. Poignant grief there is here, unanswered questioning, moments of passionate despair. But with the beautiful and thoroughly Elgarian theme at 96 begins to creep in the spirit of resignation to the inevitable, and of divine pity for human failure, born of this bitter self-discovery. From this point on is heard unmistakably the deeper note of religious consolation, reaching full expression at last in the melody marked *Molto espressivo e sostenuto*, one of the noblest, profoundest, and most spiritual that Elgar has conceived, with which the movement ends.

The finale opens with a slow introduction, intended partly to direct our attention back to the first movement and partly to forecast the strains destined to complete the cycle which it began. We hear the mysterious groping theme first heard in its development and fragments of the "Ideal." Especial emphasis is laid, however, on a marchlike tune, given out by bassoons and low strings at the sixth measure, and on an aspiring phrase for clarinet (measures 10–11) peculiar to the present movement. The prevailing mood here, both in the main theme with its emphatic interlocking rhythms (the opening Allegro) and in the second theme at 114, with its buoyant triplets recalling the finale of Brahms's third symphony, is energetic will. This seems to merge in jubilant achievement in the march-like theme of the introduction at its reëntrance at 118. For a moment, to be sure, doubt as to this triumph seems to be suggested by a rather halting version of the "Ideal" (129) and by a pondering version of the march theme (130). But with the return of the main themes of the movement at its recapitulation, beginning at 134 and now inflected towards A-flat, the radical tonality of the whole symphony, the mood of vigorous volition revives, and from now on to the splendid reassertion, by the full orchestra, in its richest sonorities, of the theme of the "Ideal," all is one long climax.

It is hard to see how any candid student can deny the greatness of this symphony. If only for the stoutness of its structure, the grasp with which the fundamental principles of musical form are seized, however the details have to be modified to suit the occasion, and for the richness and variety of its treatment of orchestral coloring, it would hold a conspicuous place among modern orchestral works. But of course these things are only means; the end of music is expression. It is, then, to the fact that the symphony gives eloquent voice to some of the deepest, most sacred, and most elusive of human feelings that we must attribute its real importance. That it does this at a time when most musicians are looking outward rather than inward, and incline to value sensuous beauty above thought, and vividness above profundity, gives us all the more reason for receiving it with gratitude, and finding in it a good omen for the future.

IV

CLAUDE DEBUSSY

CLAUDE DEBUSSY

—

O peculiarity of contemporary musical taste is more striking than the extraordinary popularity which the elusive songs and piano pieces of Debussy have enjoyed during the last decade or two. They have been heard, with a delight agreeably mixed with bewilderment, in the drawing-rooms of the whole world, just as Grieg's were at a slightly earlier period; and, like Grieg, their author has become the idol of the amateur. There is no doubt of it, Debussy has been the prime musical fad of the twentieth century. The fact is interesting — worth examination. The reasons of it throw a strong light not only on Debussy himself, but — which is more important — on our whole contemporary musical life.

Claude Achille Debussy, born in 1862 at St. Germain-en-Laye, near Paris, and educated at the Conservatoire, first gained wide fame by his opera, "Pelléas et Mélisande," produced at the Opéra Comique in 1902. By its imaginative re-creation in music of Maeterlinck's fatalism and atmosphere of mystery, by its dramatic directness, its justice of declamation, its moderation and avoidance of Wagnerian exaggeration, perhaps above all by the originality of its harmonic style and its delicately tinted orchestration, it undoubtedly marked an epoch in French music. Debussy had at this time already fixed the fundamental qualities of his style in such compositions as the quartet for strings (1893), more virile than his later works, and the well-known orchestral prelude after a prose poem by Mallarmé, archpriest of the symbolistic movement, "L'Aprèsmidi d'un faune." In later orchestral pieces, the Nocturnes for orchestra (1899), the symphonic sketches "La Mer" (1905), the highly colored "Iberia" (1907), as well as in choral works like the "Martyre de Saint Sébastien" (1911), we see him refining the same manner, seeking always, like his compatriot the poet Verlaine, the subtleties, the delicacies, the shades and half-shades, *la nuance, la nuance toujours*. It is, however, through his smaller works — his songs and especially his piano pieces — that Debussy is best known to the mass of his admirers; and as the same qualities reveal themselves here too, it is in these that we shall try to understand them. In the "Estampes" (1903), the "Masques" (1904), the "Images" (1905 and 1908), the "Préludes" (1910 and 1913), and many lesser pieces he has created what is virtually a department of his own in the literature of the piano. Here is the essential Debussy.

The adaptation between the art and the audience here, as is always the case where there is extreme popularity, is so perfect that we can equally well begin our study from either end. Let us start with the audience. Not that Debussy consciously sought to "give the public what it wants"; no artist worthy the name does that. What is meant is simply that his qualities were spontaneously such as exactly to satisfy his audience's requirements; or, in biological terms, the organism was fortunate enough to be exactly suited to its en-

vironment, peculiarly "fit to survive." As
investigating biologists we can therefore either
approach the environment through the organism or the organism through the environment —
and we choose to do the latter.

The environment of the modern composer
is a public numerically larger than ever before,
and qualitatively affected by this increased
size according to the law of averages — de-
graded, that is, from the qualities of the minority toward those of the majority. In less
abstract terms, the modern audience contains
to every one intelligent listener ten or a hundred who are ignorant, untrained, or inattentive. The results of this disproportion are
familiar to us on all sides; they range from
such a general matter as the very conception
of art, and especially of music, as a mere
amusement or diversion rather than a spiritual
experience, down to such details as the preference, natural to the untrained, of sensuous
pleasure (in rich tone-combinations, for example) to emotion and thought (as embodied
musically in melody), and of a vague day-
dreaming mood when listening to music to the

imaginative and sympathetic attention that music requires of him who would really grasp its objective beauty.

Now it is in his appeal to this modern preference of sensation to thought and emotion, and of subjective day-dreaming to the impersonal perception of beauty, that Debussy has been especially happy. He is not, of course, alone in making these appeals. The preoccupation with the sensuous is observable in most contemporary music, an especially striking instance being Strauss's orchestration. As for the ministering to "mood" rather than to the sense of beauty, the whole tendency toward "program," so characteristic of our time, might be accounted for by a cynic as a sacrifice to the majority of something they do not understand (music) to something they do (an opportunity for day-dreaming). But Debussy is peculiarly thoroughgoing in his application of these familiar modern methods. All the elements of his art are focused upon this kind of satisfaction.

First he gives us a title admirably fitted (for he has keen literary instinct) to liberate our reverizing impulse — "Gardens in the Rain," "Reflections in the Water," "Sounds and Perfumes Turn in the Evening Air," "Gold-Fish," "Veils." Then he proceeds to establish the mood of idle reverie thus suggested by means of a tonal web which at no point distracts our attention by any definite features of its own, melodic, rhythmic, harmonic, or structural. All is vague, floating, kaleidoscopic. Sustained melody is especially avoided, for nothing arrests attention or dominates mood like melody; we have therefore only bits and snippets of tune, forming and disappearing like cloud forms or the eddies in smoke-wreaths. The rhythms are equally casual and indeterminate, often of exquisite grace, but obeying no law. The harmonies are surprisingly various — rich, clear, or clangorous, as the case may be; but always elusive, avoiding the definition that would impose thought rather than encourage fancy. The effect of vagueness is here enhanced by the much-talked-of whole-tone scale. As there is little musical thought or emotion (melody), there is still less of that natural growth and combination of

thought with thought which we call thematic
development and polyphony. These are alien
to the type of art, and are wisely avoided.

It is curious to compare Debussy's treatment
of his programs with that of Strauss. The
imagination of the German, however he may
call literary or pictorial associations to his
aid, is primarily musical. A literary idea may
suggest to him a theme, as Till Eulenspiegel's
capricious mischief strikes from him that surprising Till motive, with its queer jumps and
galvanic rhythms. But once such a theme
exists it begins to act, musically, of itself, and
develops such a network of musically interesting relationships that the listener, fascinated, clean forgets the program in his
purely æsthetic delight. Strauss, probably,
forgets it too. He does for us, in spite of his
programs, exactly the kind of thing that
Mozart, Beethoven, and Schumann do; he
creates intrinsically significant and expressive
musical forms (melodies) capable of absorbing
our attention and transfiguring all they touch
— even a rogue like Till Eulenspiegel — with
their æsthetic magic. The Frenchman's im-

agination, on the contrary, is primarily literary, dramatic, pictorial. He is led by it, not to the creation of musically significant forms, but to a keenly sympathetic realization of the mood suggested by the program, and to a most subtle musical evocation of it by appropriate means, chiefly sensuous. He is thus, literally, a painter of "mood pictures." And as most people do not care to make the effort to follow and relive a musical experience, but prefer to be lulled by agreeable sounds into a trance in which their fancy may weave adventures and project pictures for itself, his audience is delighted. From this point of view symbolism is the type of art which most appeals to the inartistic, and Debussy is the musician most beloved by the unmusical.

We should not be talking about Debussy, however, if these negatives were all there were to say about him. Thousands of composers before him have succeeded in avoiding definite melody, rhythm, and harmony, coherent thematic development, and thoughtful polyphony, and have won only oblivion. His not distracting our attention by these musical elements is a part of his scheme of art, but the more important part of it is the sensuous charm by which he wins our interest and inhibits our mental and emotional activity — the sheer tonal magic of his sonorities. He is a miracle of deftness in the purveying of musical sweets. This is admitted even by his detractors, who cannot deny the seductiveness with which his music woos the physical ear, however little it appeals to their heads or their hearts. As for his admirers, they become rhapsodic over these "effects" and "sonorities," which they praise with a half-religious awe that used to be reserved for ideas. Listen, for instance, to M. Chennevière,[1] an accredited expositor: "Voluptuous, corporeal, naturalistic — such is the Debussyan art. The passions, the sentiments, leave him often indifferent." And again: "The modern ear has become very fine, very delicate. It delights in sonorities. A beautiful chord is a rare intoxication, and sometimes an author repeats it lingeringly, the better to savor it." If we

[1] "Claude Debussy et son œuvre," by Daniel Chennevière, Paris, 1913.

adopt, at least tentatively, this frankly sensuous and hedonistic view of music, we shall find much to admire in Debussy.

In the long evolution from the simple to the complex which music shares with everything else we know we may observe two different methods of tone-combination which, working together, have given us the elaborate texture of the modern art. That especially suited to melodic instruments, like those used in the orchestra or the chorus, puts melodies together as an engraver puts together lines, each remaining distinct, standing off clearly from the others, representing a different musical thought, and yet all agreeing, or, as we say, harmonizing. This method, called polyphony, requiring great skill in the composer and close attention from the audience, is illustrated by such masterpieces as a fugue of Bach, a string quartet of Beethoven, or the famous passage at the end of Wagner's Meistersinger Overture, where four themes are driven abreast as in some proud chariot. It results in a texture essentially composite, involving relations between elements held in mind together

— that is to say, it is thoughtful, and requires answering thought for its appreciation.

But as soon as the piano, ill suited to melody because of its unsustained tone, began to reach any degree of development — that is to say, about the time of Schumann (1810–1856) and Chopin (1809–1849) — it became evident that this instrument compensated for its short-comings in rendering polyphony by a special aptitude for another kind of tone-combination, which we may call the homophonic or chordal. A great many tones could be played at once, held either by the fingers or by the damper-pedal, and made to shimmer with those thou-sand hues of the tonal rainbow we call "over-tones." There was apparently no limit to the complexity of the agglomerations of tone that the ear could thus be trained not only to accept but to delight in — the rule being, as Chopin in his "fluid and vaporous sonorities" showed, that the greater in number and the more dissonant or clashing in character were these color tones, the more agreeably rich would be the resulting impression on the ear. But however complex these tone associations or chords, it is important to note that this resultant psychological impression was simple and unified — that is, the ear perceived but one thing, and not several as in the polyphonic style. There was therefore no comparison of different elements, no thought or emotion; there was simply sensation, physically delightful, mentally and emotionally meaningless.

Debussy has probably brought more talent and originality to the elaboration of this method of writing for the piano than any other composer since Chopin and Schumann. Open his pages anywhere and you will find these wide-spaced chords, these gossamer arpeggios and scales embroidering them, these nicely calculated grace-notes adding just the dissonance needed to season the dish. Take, for instance, the opening measures of "La Cathédrale engloutie" (Figure XVIII), characteristically marked "Profoundly calm (in a softly sonorous mist)."

The intention to produce a misty, not to say foggy, homogeneity of tone here is so obvious that it seems strange that just such passages have aroused the ire of pedants who

FIGURE XVIII.

From "La Cathédrale engloutie" (Préludes, Book I).

Profondément calme (Dans une brume doucement sonore).

(The incompleted ties indicate that the chord is to be kept sounding by the pedal.)

have tried to apply to them the rules of the other way of writing — the polyphonic. When we wish diverse melodies to stand out clearly one from another, we must avoid "parallel fifths and octaves," which make them coalesce. Accordingly Debussy has been blamed, by those who prefer rules to reason, for using precisely the device which will give him the physical richness with mental vacuity which he is seeking.

When this admirable colorist wishes a brighter or more incisive sonority than one of this kind, he resorts to dissonances, and especially to the interval of the "second" —

notes adjacent in the scale. The opening measures of "Et la lune descend sur le temple qui fut" (Figure XIX) afford an example of

FIGURE XIX.

"Et la lune descend sur la temple qui fut."

this in a quiet tone; more clangorous qualities of it will be found in "Masques," "L'île joyeuse," and "Jardins sous la pluie." The first example illustrates what was said of the simplicity for the mind, whatever the complexity for the ear, of this kind of tone-combination. The chords contain a good many notes each; but there emerges only one melody, and that rather obvious.

The same search for rich or brilliant color that led to this use of "seconds," carried a little further, brought the composer to that whole-tone scale (or scale entirely made up of "seconds," as C, D, E, F-sharp, G-sharp, A-sharp, C) which he has used with such irresistible appeal. He has, to be sure, no patent right in it. Moussorgsky, Borodine, and others had used it before him; his French contemporaries have used it with skill; and now that it is common property some have even elicited from it strains of plangent force and manly energy foreign to Debussy's temperament. The fact remains that he has made it peculiarly his own by the subtlety, variety, and charm of his employment of it, as may be seen, for example, throughout "Voiles," in the first book of Préludes, and in scattered measures in almost any of his pieces. The whole-tone scale is indeed preordained by nature as a goal to which such an art as Debussy's inevitably tends; its clashing tones feed the greedy ear with the richest diet the gamut can provide; at the same time the equivocal character of the chords, or rather the single chord (the so-called "augmented triad") that can harmonize it, and the self-contradictoriness of its tones from the point of view of the older scale, do away with the sense of key and even of momentary repose, and leave us groping in a tonal night in which, since there is nothing to be observed, we can give ourselves up undisturbed to dreaming.

Debussy is thus a true child of his time in his quest of the sensuous, and a true child of his country in the subtlety with which he pursues it. His Gallic taste saves him from the coarseness of so much of the contemporary Teutonic art; and while his aim is no more spiritual than that of the Germans, he prefers innuendo, implication, and understatement to the gross exaggeration of Strauss, the vehemence in platitude of Mahler, and the plodding literalness of Reger. Thus opposing, as he has so effectively done, the ideal of mere force, reducing in "Pelléas" the mammoth modern orchestra to a handful of men skillfully exploited, substituting the most elusive sonorities of the piano for the crashing magnificence of the Liszt school, everywhere insisting on subtle quality rather than overwhelming quantity, he has exercised one of the most beneficial of influences against vulgarity of the bumptious type. But sybaritism, too, has its own vulgarity; the question of aim is fundamental in art; and in judging the distinction of Debussy's aims we cannot evade the question whether physical pleasure, however refined, is the highest good an artist can seek. His charm, beyond doubt, is great enough to justify his popularity. Yet it would be regrettable if the student of modern French music, satisfied with this charm, were to neglect the less popular but more virile, more profound, and more spiritual music of César Franck, Ernest Chausson, and Vincent d'Indy.

NOTE: Claude Debussy died in Paris, March 26, 1918.

V

VINCENT D'INDY

—

Vincent d'Indy as a Young Man

V

VINCENT D'INDY

I

OUR age, because of the natural failure of our inner powers, at first, to keep pace with the recent unprecedented increase of our external resources, will probably be known to the future as one of unparalleled confusion. With the mental and moral habits and the nervous systems inherited from a more placid generation, we find ourselves plunged in this maelstrom produced by cheap printing, quick communication, and facile transportation. Prepared to digest only a limited environment, we are fed the whole world. No wonder we are distracted. . . . The situation, of course, is full of interest to the more adventurous temperaments; but however stimulating to the man of action it is scarcely favorable to the artist, since art is born only of tranquil emotion, firmly grasped and clearly arranged. Most contemporary musicians are thus bewildered and to some extent defeated by the very richness of the materials at hand; their art is not equal to the strain put upon it by their greatly enlarged resources; and their music is in consequence unindividual in expression, flabbily eclectic in style, and vague or wandering in structure.

It may seem at first thought paradoxical that these melancholy results of a momentary insufficiency of the mind to its materials should have proved most fatal precisely in the country that in simpler times has done most to create music. Strange it is, indeed, that Germany, which in Beethoven voiced the spiritual aspiration, in Schumann the romantic joy, and in Brahms the philosophic meditation of the whole world, should find itself at length reduced to the half-impotent strivings of a Mahler, to the learned lucubrations of a Reger, while mixed with even the gold of its one genius, Strauss, there should be so much dross of cheap sensationalism and irrelevant melodrama. Yet to consideration these signs of a widespread decadence in

German music will not by any means remain incomprehensible. For it will be seen that the Teutonic introspectiveness, the supreme gift of that temperament, incomparable and sufficient endowment as it seemed in the musicians of the great period, hardly suffices those who have to steer their way in a much more complicated environment, surrounded by pitfalls, calling at every step for qualities with which the typical German is by no means so well supplied — intelligence, discrimination, moderation, and taste. It is the lack of these intellectual or spiritual qualities, rather than any falling off in purely emotional power, that has brought the great stream of music that flowed through Bach, Beethoven, Schumann, and Brahms to its end in the stagnant morasses of contemporary Kapellmeistermusik, or scattered it in the showy but unsatisfying jets of sensationalism. And as Russia still remains a bit barbaric, England a little provincial, America immature, and Italy tainted with operaticism (an ugly word for an ugly thing), it is chiefly in France, with its racial genius of lucid intelligence, that we find a truly vital contemporary music. There we owe it chiefly to the high creative genius of César Franck, Belgian by birth and temperament, French in education and intellectual clarity, and to the loyal co-labors, creative, critical, and educational, of his pupils and disciples. If there is to-day, despite the confusions of the time, a clear tradition and a hopeful future for instrumental music, it is chiefly these modern Frenchmen that we have to thank.

Especially has Vincent d'Indy, to-day dominant in the group, contributed to its work for many years the indefatigable efforts of his powerful and many-sided personality, more variously gifted than any of the others, since he is not only a composer of genius, but a lucid writer, an able organizer, and a teacher and conductor of singular magnetism. He came under the influence of Franck at his most plastic period; he was a youth of twenty-two when, in 1873, he entered Franck's organ class at the Paris Conservatoire; and of the circumstances, characteristic of both teacher and pupil, under which this most fruitful relationship began, he has himself written in his "Life of Franck."

"Having with great trouble," he says, "got upon paper a formless quartet for piano and strings, I asked Franck for an appointment. When I had played him the first movement, he remained a moment silent, and then, turning toward me with a sad air, he said to me words I have never forgotten, since they had a decisive action on my life: 'There are good things here, energy, a certain instinct for dialogue of the parts, . . . the ideas are not bad, . . . but that is not enough, it is not made, and, in short, *you know nothing at all.*' Returning home in the night (the interview had taken place very late in the evening) I said to myself, in my wounded vanity, that Franck must be a reactionary, understanding nothing of youthful, modern art. Nevertheless, calmer the next morning, I took up my unhappy quartet and recalled one by one his observations, . . . and I was obliged to admit that he was right: I knew absolutely nothing. I went then, almost trembling, to ask him to accept me as a pupil."

At this time Franck, already fifty-one years old, was little appreciated as a composer, appeared to the world as a hard-worked organist who taught ten hours a day and wrote for two hours before breakfast works seldom heard, and had indeed not yet discovered the vein from which he so enriched music during the last ten years of his life. Nevertheless d'Indy at once recognized the fruitfulness of his ideas, devoted himself to a severe technical discipline in accordance with them, and assumed that rôle of filial defender and expositor of them in which he has never wearied from that day to this. There is something not only rarely beautiful in itself, but most characteristic of the purity of d'Indy's self-forgetful devotion to music, in the loyalty which he has always given to his "Pater seraphicus," as Franck's artistic sons called him, from the period when as a student he left the conservatory which misprized his master, to the day when, himself a master, he published his "Life of Franck." M. Romain Rolland gives us a picture of it in his description of the first performance, in March, 1888, of Franck's

"Theme, fugue, and variation" for harmonium and piano, at a concert of the *Société nationale de musique*, when Franck played the harmonium, and d'Indy the piano. "I always remember," says M. Rolland,[1] "his respectful attitude toward the old musician, his studious care to follow his indications: one would have thought he was a pupil, attentive and docile; and this was touching from a young master, established by so many works — the *Chant de la Cloche*, *Wallenstein*, the *Symphonie sur un thème montagnard* — and perhaps better known and more popular than César Franck himself. Since then twenty years have passed; I continue to see him as I saw him that evening; and whatever happens now his image will remain always for me closely associated with that of the great master dominating, with a paternal smile, this small assembly of faithful ones."

This "small assembly of faithful ones," the pupils of Franck, such as Duparc, Chausson, Coquard, Bordes, Ropartz, Benoit, d'Indy, as well as others, like Saint-Saëns and Fauré,

---

[1] Musiciens d'aujourd'hui; Romain Rolland.

who, though not his pupils, have felt his influence, have virtually created since 1870, largely under his inspiration, a new music in France. The story of it may be read in M. Rolland's book, in the essay "Le renouveau." At the time of the Franco-Prussian War (in which d'Indy served as a corporal of the 105th regiment), symphonic and chamber music suffered almost complete neglect in Paris. "Before 1870," writes M. Saint-Saëns,[1] "a French composer who had the folly to venture into the domain of instrumental music, had no other way to get his works played than to organize a concert himself, inviting his friends and the critics. The rare chamber music societies were as much closed to all new comers as the orchestral concerts; their programs contained only the celebrated names, above discussion, of the great classic symphonists. At that time one had truly to be bereft of all common sense to write music. It was in order to correct this state of things that a group of musicians organized in February, 1871, the *Société nationale de musique*,

[1] *Harmonie et Melodie.* C. Saint-Saëns.

with the device 'Ars gallica,' and the avowed
end of 'aiding the production and familiariza-
tion of all serious musical works, of French
composers, and of encouraging, so far as may
be in its power, all musical tentatives, of
whatever kind, which show on the part of
their author elevated and artistic aspirations.'"
M. Rolland does not hesitate to call the *Société
nationale* "the cradle and the sanctuary of
French art." "All that has been great in
French music from 1870 to 1900," he says,
"has come by way of it. Without it the
greater part of the works which are the honor
of our music not only would not have been
performed, but perhaps would not even have
been written." And he draws from the programs records of the performance of important
compositions by Franck, Saint-Saëns, d'Indy,
Chabrier, Lalo, Bruneau, Chausson, Debussy,
Dukas, Lekeu, Magnard, and Ravel.

Vincent d'Indy's personal contribution to
the work of the society began to be considerable from 1881 on, when the influence of the
Franck school became dominant. In 1886
his proposal to include in the programs the

works of classic and foreign composers led to the resignation of Saint-Saëns and Bussine. In 1890, at the death of Franck, he became president of the society. Under his influence the representation of classical works has particularly increased — Palestrina, Vittoria, Josquin, Bach, Handel, Rameau, Gluck, as well as Beethoven, Schumann, Liszt, Brahms. Foreign contemporary music has been represented chiefly by Strauss, Grieg, and the Russians. In recent years the *Société nationale* has been charged with taking on too exclusive a character, especially with guarding the traditional at the expense of the new; and the *Société musicale indépendante* has been founded by some of the younger men as a protest.

In 1900 d'Indy became president of the Schola Cantorum, founded six years earlier by Charles Bordes, Alexandre Guilmant, and himself, primarily for the cultivation of the church music based on the Gregorian chant. In his discourse of inauguration he explained his purpose of enlarging the function of the school to cover all musical instruction; and while characteristically insisting that the means to renovate modern music were to be found in the study of "the decorative art of the plain chant, the architectural art of the Palestrina period, and the expressive art of the great Italians of the seventeenth century," yet promised to take his students "through the same path that art has followed, so that, undergoing in their period of study the transformations music has undergone through the centuries, they will emerge from it so much the better armed for the modern combat, in that they will have lived, so to speak, the life of art, and will have assimilated in their natural order the forms which have logically succeeded each other in the different epochs of artistic development." Both in the special leaning toward the music of the church which his devout and somewhat mystical temperament here suggested, and in the broad eclecticism with which his intelligence insisted on combining it, he showed clearly the influence of his master César Franck, whom indeed he asserted to be in a sense "the grandfather of this Schola Cantorum, since it is his system of teaching that we endeavor to continue and apply here." Like his master he wished to cultivate in his students both a solid learning, without which nothing vital can be contributed to art, and the enthusiasm without which it degenerates into pedantry. To understand the great influence for good exerted on French music by the Schola, we need only recall d'Indy's description of "the noble teaching of César Franck, founded on Bach and Beethoven, but admitting besides all enthusiasms, all new and generous aspirations." [1]

In the sixteen years that d'Indy has been at the head of the Schola Cantorum he has accomplished an amount of unselfish labor for the advancement of music that would have been extraordinary under any circumstances, and becomes almost incredible when we remember that in the same period he has produced over half a dozen original works of the first importance. He is indeed a man of unusual physical, nervous, and mental strength, accustomed to indefatigable labor. Thus in addition to all his teaching he organ-

[1] *César Franck*, by Vincent d'Indy.

izes operatic performances and choral, orchestral, and chamber-music concerts; he conducts,
and teaches others to conduct; he edits the
classics — Rameau, Destouches, Solomon de
Rossi — and the folk-songs of his native mountains of the Vivarais; he gives lectures and
makes studies of the predecessors of Beethoven,
of Franck; he writes criticisms for the monthly
press; and, most serviceable of all perhaps to
distant students, he describes the principles of
his art in a masterly and exhaustive treatise,
the "Cours de composition musicale," unfortunately not yet translated into English.

And all this is only his winter work. In
the summer he retires to his château of Faugs,
near the little mountain village of Boffres,
in Ardèche, and there, in a room in the tower,
whence on a clear day he can see Mt. Blanc,
he composes the works in which these principles are so nobly exemplified. Besides the
early "Chant de la Cloche," by which he won
the grand prize of the city of Paris in 1885 and
first established his reputation, he has written
three other large choral works: the two operas
"Fervaal" (1895) and "L'Etranger" (1901),

and the oratorio "La Légende de St. Christophe," recently completed. For orchestra, aside from the early trilogy of symphonic poems "Wallenstein," over-Wagnerian in inspiration, and other early or lesser works, there are four masterpieces of the first order: "Istar," symphonic variations, 1896; the second Symphony, in B flat, 1904; the symphony, "Un Jour d'Été à la Montagne," 1905; and the symphonic poem "Souvenirs," written to the memory of his wife, 1906. This incomplete list may be finished with three equally masterly chamber-music pieces: the second String Quartet, E major, 1897; the Violin Sonata, 1904, and the Piano Sonata, 1907 — not to mention the youthful Piano Quartet of 1878, or the delightful Trio for Clarinet, Violoncello, and Piano of 1887.

What, then, are these fundamental principles of composition which d'Indy has insisted upon in his teaching, promulgated in the "Cours de composition musicale," and exemplified in his works? They are all, in essence, but differing forms of the central principle of all art, of all beauty — that the

utmost variety must be but the outgrowth
and flowering of a perfect unity. We have
seen that many modern composers, baffled
by the richness of the materials with which
they had to deal, have failed in the effort
thus to stamp unity upon them : their art
has been confused and fragmentary. Others
again — the pseudo-classics and reactionaries
— have resorted to a violent simplification of
the material in order to preserve unity, and
have thus impoverished their art. Only the
greatest, in the first rank of whom must be
placed Franck and d'Indy, have had at once
a firm enough hold upon musical tradition
and a broad enough command of new methods
and idioms to write music at once various
and unified, at once thoroughly "modern"
and thoroughly sane. To this unifying power
of d'Indy's mind M. Rolland pays a fine
tribute. "Clearness!" he cries, "it is the mark
of M. d'Indy's intelligence. There are no
shadows in him. His thought and his art are
as clear as his look, which gives to his face so
much of youth. It is a necessity for him to
judge, to order, to classify, to unify. Never

was there a spirit more French. . . . And this is the more remarkable in that his nature is far from being simple. Through a wide musical education, a constant desire to learn, it has been enriched by many elements, different, almost contradictory. . . . Not to be submerged by this richness of opposing elements requires a great force of passion or of will, which eliminates or chooses and transforms. M. d'Indy eliminates almost nothing: he organizes. There are in his music the qualities of a general: the knowledge of the end, the patient will to attain it, the perfect acquaintance with the means, the spirit of order, and the mastery over his work and over himself. Despite the variety of the materials he employs, the whole is always clear."

II

If we examine, as typical of d'Indy's mature style, a passage such as the introduction to the slow movement of the B flat Symphony, shown in Figure XX, we are struck at once by the complexity of the detail — the bold unexpectedness of the melodic lines, the chromatic harmony, the constantly varying rhythms — and by the perfect final clearness with which it nevertheless impresses us, so that each note seems inevitable and the whole unmistakable in meaning. It is this com-

FIGURE XX.

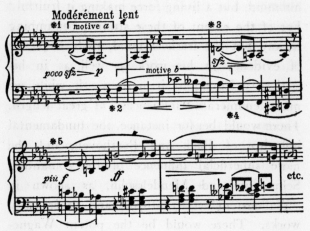

bination of complexity and simplicity, characteristic more or less of all really great modern composers but perhaps to a peculiar degree of d'Indy, that we have to analyze and account for to ourselves in some detail if we would thoroughly understand his music. What is the mysterious power in him that enables him to give so distinctly personal a stamp to elements drawn from so many sources? What is the unifying principle in all this variety? What lifts this insatiable student above his studies, and renders his knowledge not a dead lumber weighing down his mind, but a living force making it fruitful? For of the extent of these studies, benumbing to any but the freshest mind, there is plenty of evidence in his work as well as in his critical writings; if it were worth while we might enumerate "influences" at great length. There would be, for instance, the fundamental influence of Bach and Beethoven, and the more superficial influence of the romantics, Schumann and Mendelssohn, as shown in "Wallenstein" (1873–1879), and other early works. There would be the potent Wagnerian influence, of which "Fervaal" is the chief monument, although it appears in all that he has written; and there would be the even more pervasive and inspiring influence of his master, Franck. We should have to take account, too, of the reflection, especially in later works like the piano sonata, the violin sonata, and the second symphony, of the harmonic idiom of Debussy and other contemporaries, the whole-tone scale, and the like. And under these individual influences we should find more general, subtle, and pervasive ones, we should find the great communal streams of the French folk-song and the Gregorian plain chant. Yet all these streams, and others too many to mention, have been gathered up into one clear personality. What has been the transmuting magic?

The composer himself suggests the answer in several passages that may here be brought together.

"It is perfectly logical," he writes in *Mercure de France*,[1] "and in the order of things that, when a man of genius shows himself in one country, the artists of the other nations try to assimilate his processes. I see nothing reprehensible in that, and this international free trade even appears to me one of the vital conditions of the development of art. . . .

[1] Inquest on the influence of Germany, especially of Wagner, on French music, January, 1903.

Moreover, can the artist ever, in spite of all influences, give anything else than the art that he carries in himself?"

"You ask me," he says to an interviewer of the *Revue Bleue*,[1] "to define French music. In reality there is no French music, and in general there is no national music. There is *music*, which is of no country; there are musical masterpieces, which belong to no one nation." He is led on to an interesting comparison of our period, in its desire for greater simplicity, with the end of the sixteenth century, and the illuminating statement: "M. Debussy is a little our Monteverde; he abandons melody for recitative, for 'the representative style,' as they said in the first years of the seventeenth century; he renounces the resources of counterpoint, he even foregoes modulation." But when the interviewer, seeking to entrap him into condemnation of his contemporary which would make good copy, asks, "And do you not desire rather the triumph of melody and polyphony?" he replies:

[1] "Revue Politique et Littéraire" (*Revue Bleue*), March 26, 1904.

"I have but one desire; it is that they write beautiful things." The third passage is one of the axioms that he gives to his students at the Schola Cantorum: "All processes are good, on condition that they never become the principal end, but are regarded only as means for making music." And finally he makes his meaning even more definite in a discussion of M. Roger Ducasse:[1] "I am sure that when M. Ducasse is willing to trust himself more to the impulses of his heart rather than to researches in sonorities, he will be able to make very beautiful music. There is in art, truly, nothing but the heart that can produce beauty — (*Il n'est vraiment, en art, que le cœur pour engendrer de la beauté*)."

Yes, it is his heart that guides his mind through the mazes of its knowledge; it is his luminous sincerity that shines through all he writes, however complex it may be in detail; both the warmth and the light of his music come from his emotion. Responsive emotion in the listener, accordingly, is the key to the intricacies of his style. If we attend to the

[1] *Revue Musicale S. I. M.*, February 15, 1913.

letter only we are baffled, bewildered: there
are so many notes, such queer progressions,
in that passage from the symphony, for example. But if we hearken for the spirit, all
becomes clear, and strangely moving. It is
waxing and waning feeling, a wave of emotion,
that expresses itself in that rise to the strident
B of the fourth measure and in the subsequent
hesitating descent. And as emotion is the
motive force of the whole, emotion it is also
that explains the details.

Take for instance the very texture of the
melody. We note two contrasting figures
or motives, one, which we may call *a*, melancholy or at least contemplative, characterized
by the fall of a fourth, and another, *b*, in
which the more vigorous rise of a seventh
gives a sense of opposing will. The whole
passage is wrought from these two contrasting yet mutually supplementing strands with
singular concentration. There is not a note,
save the chords in the last two measures, that
does not belong to one or the other. There
is something relentless in such insistence.
The grip is not relaxed for a moment. The

thought is hammered in. The music throbs
like a pulse. Yet there is in this insistence
nothing of the monotony of mere repetition;
the feeling never stagnates. On the contrary,
each assertion accumulates fresh force, the
emotion rises by its own expression, and there
is ordered, purposeful, relentless progression.
Thus motive *a* is stated first from D flat;
then, at *3, from D, higher and louder; then,
at *5, from E flat but this time fairly carried
off its feet by its oppugnant fellow, *b*. Similarly *b*, first heard quietly, almost timidly, in
the bass, in the key of D flat, at *2, is repeated
at *4 more firmly and in the key of D minor,
making it in the main higher than before
though starting on the same note; finally it
appears in the treble, as just stated, at *5, and
rises as in a passionate cry to the B, whence it
slowly subsides. In short, we see here a
"logic of emotion" quite as absolute as that
of the reason, and far more appropriate to
music, in which mere reason must be content
with a subordinate place. As always in the
best music, the logic of emotion involves
both the fundamental unity of the motives

(since no emotion would amount to much if it was so weak that it forgot what it was about) and their gradual cumulative growth in diversity as they realize themselves in expression. Even d'Indy's music is not always so true to the logic of emotion as this, as we shall have occasion later to notice; even Homer nods; but the motival variety in unity of all good melody, as a result of its emotional origin, is none the less ineluctable as a principle.

Looking again at the passage we may note more specifically the interest, vitality, and flexibility of its rhythms. This is again, as in all the composer's best work, ultimately due to truth to emotion. Motive *b* occurs three times, but never twice the same. The second time, at *4, it enters earlier in the measure than before, as if impatient, and ends with the persistent tramp of quarter notes. The third time it strikes in almost roughly (*5), its second and third notes are displaced — syncopated — by agitation, while its last three notes, comprising the crisis and its subsidence, are lengthened out from a half measure to a measure and a half. (See

Figure XXI.) We see thus exemplified the basic principles of expression through rhythm, the hastening or compression of the phrase in response to passion, its retardation or expansion with returning calm. "Expression,"

FIGURE XXI.

First state

Second state

Third state

writes d'Indy,[1] "consists in the translation of sentiments and impressions, by the aid of certain characteristic modifications, affecting the rhythmic, melodic, and harmonic forms of the musical discourse. . . . *Agogique*, consisting in the modifications of the rhythmic movement, — precipitation, slackening, regular and irregular interruptions, etc. — has for its effect to render the relative impressions of *calm* and *agitation*."

[1] *Cours de Composition Musicale*, Book I, page 123.

Such a conception of rhythm, emphasizing its sensitive fluctuation in response to mood, and demanding of the artist complete sincerity and flexibility of expression, is at the pole from the conventional notion of it as an almost mechanical balancing of equal sections of melody, cut off so to speak with a yardstick. D'Indy leaves his readers in no doubt as to his opinion of all such conventional sing-song, the doggerel of music. "To beat the time and to give the rhythm of a musical phrase," he says,[1] "are two completely distinct operations, often opposed. The coincidence of the rhythm and the measure is an entirely particular case, which men have unfortunately tried to generalize, propagating the error that 'the first beat of the measure is always strong.' This identification of rhythm with measure has had the most deplorable consequences for music. . . . Rhythm, submitted to the restricting requirements of meter, becomes rapidly impoverished, even to the most desolating platitude, just as a branch of a tree, strongly

[1] *Cours*, I, 27.

compressed by a ligature, becomes enfeebled and atrophied, while its neighbors absorb all the sap." [1] Again: "In the seventeenth century the bar-line ceased to be simply a graphic sign; it became a periodic starting point for the rhythm, which it soon robbed of all its liberty and elegance. Hence come those symmetrical and square-cut forms to which we owe a great part of the platitudes of the Italianism of the eighteenth and nineteenth centuries." [2] Finally, summing the whole matter up in a sentence: "The *carrure* [that is, square-cut phrase-balance, symmetry by measures, narrowly limited to the number 4 and its multiples] is an element of vulgarity, rarely useful outside of certain special forms of dance music." [3]

The vulgarity of the *carrure*, of sing-song, as we may call it in English, is due, it cannot be too much insisted upon, to the mental and emotional inertia, the thoughtlessness, the surrender to the mechanism of habit,

---

[1] See the present writer's paper on "The Tyranny of the Bar-line," New Music Review, December, 1909.

[2] *Cours*, I, 217.   [3] *Cours*, I, 40.

of which it is the product and the index. It proceeds from a conventionality essentially unspontaneous, uncreative, a conventionality that permits the length and shape of the phrase to be imposed by convenience, ease, and precedent rather than by the emotion it ought to incarnate. Hence singsong is found not only in all music which, like so-called "popular songs," emanates from trivial people or from people only superficially moved, but also in the music even of sincere composers in their moments of inattention, pretentiousness, or routine. Even so fine a composer as Elgar is frequently banal in rhythm. On the other hand, deeply felt work always spontaneously assumes individual rhythmic outlines; and undoubtedly such free and unstereotyped outlines, though to the initiated listener they constitute one of its most potent and lasting beauties, and thus are an essential condition of its longevity, repel at first by their apparent eccentricity or "obscurity" the uninitiated and the inattentive, and thus postpone its general acceptance. Thus the attribution to d'Indy of "dryness" and "lack of melody" which one sometimes hears may be taken as an inverted tribute to the spontaneity of his melody and especially of his rhythms. Only one who did not feel sympathetically the wide ground swell of those phrases from the symphony could find them groping or uncertain because they did not fall into exactly four measures. The moment one felt the coördinating force of their fresh personal emotion one would not regret the absence of the conventional strait-jackets.

It is emotion again that explains his attitude toward harmony. Just as he is ahead of most of his contemporaries in the fundamental and surprisingly neglected matter of rhythm, because he conceives it as so flexible an instrument of expression, so he is rather at odds with many of them, especially with the impressionist school in his own country, on the much studied — perhaps over-studied — question of harmony, because he conceives harmony as primarily expressive, while they conceive it as primarily sensuous.[1] A clue

[1] Compare what is said of Debussy, for example, above, page 143.

to his attitude is that sentence of his in criticism of Ducasse: "I am sure that when
M. Ducasse is willing to trust himself more
to the impulses of his heart rather than to
researches in sonorities, he will be able to
make very beautiful music." "Researches
in sonorities" — that is, in the minds of the
group of French composers led by Debussy,
almost a synonym for harmony; what they
ask of harmony is combinations of tone delicious to the physical ear: subtly, delicately
delicious, no doubt, and to a highly refined
ear, but still aiming consciously at the ear
rather than at the mind or the heart. The
means of satisfying such a desire being sensations, aural sensations ingeniously built up
and combined, they have rightly concentrated
their attention on the single moment of merged
sounds — the chord — rather than on the
procession of separate sounds — the melody,
and its relation to other melodies sounding
with it. "Accord," "sonorité" — these are
the slogans of the impressionists.

To d'Indy, on the other hand, harmony,
like all the other technical elements of music, is

primarily a means of expression, and therefore results rather from the confluence of
melodies, themselves dictated by emotion,
than from the adjustment of sonorities to
please the ear. One has only to look again
at the passage from the symphony to see how
such an attitude works out in practise. There
is no preoccupation here with "effect"; the
harmony, one might almost say, receives no
attention for itself, but is solely a result of
the melodic movements; yet so free and expressive are these movements, so truly conceived to voice the emotions behind them,
and combined with such art, that this resultant harmony is far more poignant, far more
fresh and unexpected and striking than if it
had been confected for itself alone. And
this is natural and easily comprehensible,
since we should not expect any amount of
ingenuity spent on the single chord to achieve
the results that melodies, feeling out into the
unknown, easily attain. Such an attitude
toward harmony requires, it is true, a certain
daring: you cannot swim with your feet on
the ground; but the freedom of movement

you get by trusting yourself to the waves amply compensates your faith.

This melodic conception of harmony has always been a fundamental characteristic of d'Indy's style, as examples from widely sundered periods will easily show. The first, Figure XXII, is a bit from the Chant Elégiaque in the early Trio for Clarinet, Cello, and Piano (1887). The charming unexpectedness

FIGURE XXII.

From Chant Elégiaque, in Trio for Clarinet, Cello, and Piano.

of the twist back into E major is thorough d'Indy, as is also the use of a persistent figure (given to the cello in the original) and the rhythmic modification of this same figure to provide the bass in the second measure. The second passage, shown in Figure XXIII, dates from thirty years later, and appears in "Souvenirs" (1906). Here again the melo-

FIGURE XXIII.
From "Souvenirs."

dies "find a way," and a more interesting, vista-opening way than any sonorities could suggest. Such passages enable us to get the full sense of what their composer means when he writes: "The study of chords *for themselves* is, from the musical point of view, an absolute æsthetic error, for harmony springs from melody, and ought never to be separated from it in its application. . . . There is only one chord, the perfect chord [triad], alone consonant, because it alone gives the sense of repose or equilibrium. All the combinations that people call 'dissonant chords,' necessitating, in order to be examined, an artificial arrest in the melodies that constitute them, have no proper existence, since in making abstraction of the movement that engenders them, one suppresses their unique reason for being. Chords have too often become the end of music; they ought never to be anything but a means, a consequence, a phenomenon essentially transient." [1] It may be held that d'Indy sometimes goes too far in his denunciations of harmonic theories based on the conception of the "chord," as for example in his note on the famous opening phrase of "Tristan and Isolde." It may also be justly remarked that his own method is not always happy in its results — that the way his melodies find is sometimes an obscure and wandering, or an unnatural and forced way. Nevertheless it remains on the whole true that on the one hand the chord conception of harmony has been responsible for a vast mass of

[1] *Cours*, I, 91 and 116.

pedantry, and has paralyzed and hamstrung whole generations of students, and that on the other hand it favors the purely sensuous trifling with tones of which there is so much in our day; while the best pages of Bach, Beethoven, Brahms, Wagner, Franck, d'Indy show a thousand beauties and poignancies which without the help of melody could never have been discovered.

In the course of Kaito's prophecy, in "Fervaal," there is a deeply moving passage to the words: "Only Death, baleful Death, shall summon Life," which strikingly illustrates its composer's way of making all the elements of music contribute to expression (see Figure XXIV). Here the upward inflection of the voice, the strange intervals, the vague harmonies, the halting movement, even the sighing syncopation of the bass, all contribute to the interpretation of the opening lines. But above all, how inexplicably stirring is the gradual increase of force and rise of pitch up to the clear chord of D major (note the composer's indication, "Clair") at the word "Life" ("Vie")! Gloom and mystery give

FIGURE XXIV.

place to hope, faith, will, to which the ecclesiastical harmonies lend an unmistakable religious coloring. This change, completely spontaneous in effect, is dictated by an art that conceals itself, and introduces us to one of the most individual features of d'Indy's harmonic technique, his ease of modulation. In his *Cours de Composition Musicale* he has worked out his theories of the expressive use of modulation with characteristic thoroughness, and with unprecedented amplitude of detail. To resume his points here, however, interesting as they are, would take us too deeply into technical matters, especially as our main interest is now in his application rather than in his statement of them. The essential principles may therefore be briefly summarized, in his own words, as follows :

(1) "Expression is the unique reason for being of modulation."

(2) "Modulation operates by a displacement of the tonic ['key-note'], by its oscillation towards the higher fifths [that is, towards the sharper keys, as to G, D, A, etc., from C] or towards the lower fifths [that is, towards the flatter keys, as to F, B flat, E flat, etc., from C]."

(3) "Modulation has for its effect to render relative impressions of brightness [that is, movement towards sharper keys produces

'*éclaircissement*'] or of darkness [movement towards flatter keys produces '*assombrissement*'].''

(4) "Modulation can never be the *end* of music, since it is by its very nature a *means* put *at the service of the musical idea.* Every modulation which has not this character of subordination to the idea is thereby inopportune, useless, and even injurious to the equilibrium of the composition." [1]

Looking back at our examples in the light of these principles, and especially with the illumination afforded by the text in Kaito's contrast of death and life, we shall find a further element of art to admire in them — their expressive use of modulation. The slow movement of the symphony begins in the comparatively "dark" key of D flat, but touches in the fourth measure, at the acme of the climax, the brighter D major, whence with the waning emotion it subsides to the original key. The passage cited from the *Chant élégiaque* emerges from the shades of E flat minor to the bright daylight of E major

[1] *Cours,* Book I, pp. 126 and 132; Book II, Part I, p. 245.

(wherein starts a new statement of the main theme). The fragment from "Souvenirs" commences in quiet grief, in the clear but rather subdued key of A minor; with the third measure a downward inflection, a sort of depression of mood, sinks it to hopeless groping in the glooms of G flat and C flat, whence it again struggles forth to new assertion, in A minor, in the phrase that follows our excerpt. Stated in bald technical terms like these, such changes may seem crude, obvious, mechanical; but anyone who will listen sympathetically to the music in which they are embodied by a master will realize the infinite variety and subtlety of their appeal.

A later appearance of this same theme in "Souvenirs," in which for the first two notes in the second measure is substituted a triplet, F, G, E, suggests the further remark that even ornament, so apt to be used merely for show, is employed by d'Indy, like so many more basic resources, singly for expression. His somewhat severe conception of art — there is much in his style that, especially in contrast with German sensuousness, is austere, bare,

almost stark — leads him to condemn superficial decoration. "The *fioriture* of the Italian dramatic school of the early nineteenth
century," he insists, "intended only to display the vocal agility of the singer (just as the
Variation of Chopin, although more musical,
puts forward the fingers of the pianist), this
fioriture, consisting usually of embroideries
about an arpeggio, is truly more harmonic
than melodic — and even the harmony is
usually extremely banal. The characteristic of the accomplished and conscientious
artist is a firm will to treat only subjects
that have a value in themselves, not borrowed from the apparel in which they are
dressed up." [1] And he elsewhere succinctly
defines the Italian *fioriture* as "that art which
consists in making heard the greatest number
of useless notes in the shortest space of
time." [2] But he takes pains to distinguish
"this surcharge dictated by bad taste" from
the more essential ornament used in the "expressive vocalises of J. S. Bach and his contemporaries, which, like the Gregorian Varia-

[1] *Cours*, Book II, Part I, pp. 454, 452.   [2] *Cours*, II, I, 165.

tion from which they derive, form a part of the melody." And he cites with approval melodies like the theme of the Allegretto in Franck's Symphony, in which a short phrase is repeated not literally but with ornamental variation resulting from the natural progression of the thought or feeling — from what, in short, we have called the logic of emotion. Such treatment is almost a mannerism in his own work. Other instances, besides the place in "Souvenirs" just cited, are the first theme of the violin sonata, the fugato in the first movement of the quartet, the main theme of the same movement, and the main theme of "Evening" in the "Summer Day on the Mountain" (Figure XXVII, *a*).

Finally, even in the matter of orchestration, the least essential of any we have considered, d'Indy is still guided by the same principle — truth to feeling. Though universally acknowledged, even by those who dislike his music, to be one of the greatest living masters of the resources of the orchestra, he never uses these resources, as does for example Rimsky-Korsakoff, in a spirit of sheer virtuosity. Nothing in his scores is put there to dazzle or to stun; all is for eloquent musical speech; and when there is great liveliness or brilliancy, as there often is — at the end of "Istar," for instance, in the scherzo of the B-flat symphony, and in "Dawn" of the "Summer Day on the Mountain" — it is in response not to an opportunity for display, but to a mood. The sharp contrast of the general method of scoring with Wagner's, especially in a composer so largely indebted to Wagner, is highly instructive in this regard. Wagner in his love of rich sonorities almost habitually doubles different groups of instruments on a single melody; d'Indy prefers the single group, not only for its superior clarity but even more, one must think, for the greater eloquence of its individual voice. The passage quoted from the symphony is a good sample of his methods. First violins on their G strings for the opening phrase, sounding at once the right note of earnestness. Bass clarinet alone on motive *b*. Both first and second violins for the more emphatic repetition of the main motive, and the low strings in

their more impassioned accents for the reiteration of the bass clarinet phrase. Then all
the violins and the violas for the third, culminating statement, — the first violins leaving
off with the B flat, the seconds with the A,
and the violas, in their more veiled tones, alone
carrying the phrase down to its final A flat.

Thus does d'Indy use the various elements of musical technique — melody, rhythm,
harmony, modulation, and even ornament
and orchestration — in the interests of emotion. Before asking whether the same
principle that we thus see so multifariously
at work in short sections of his music
can also be traced in the marshaling of its
larger masses, let us take one final example
of its operation within conveniently narrow
limits. In Figure XXV (pages 198, 199) is
shown the coda of the first movement of the
string quartet in E major, his masterpiece in
chamber music. It is entirely derived from
the fragment of Gregorian chant used as a text.
We may note summarily the following points,
which by no means exhaust the interest of the
passage.

1. Melodic. There is no salient phrase which is not derived from the root motive. As for the variety, the reader will judge for himself. This is a supreme case of the germinating power of a musical thought.

FIGURE XXV.

Coda of the first movement of the String Quartet in E, opus 45 (1897), based on the fragment from a Gregorian chant:

2. Rhythmic. The original nucleus of the theme is rhythmed mainly in quarter notes. It is reduced to even eighth notes at the beginning of the coda, and in that murmuring,

inconspicuous form stays on a dead level, so to speak, and makes a colorless background of accompaniment whence the more passionate main phrases detach themselves sharply. Beginning in the fifth measure the second violin sounds an *augmented* form of the motive (whole notes), in expression tentative, timid. This recurs in the viola in measure 11, with more of emphasis, and is broken in upon by a *syncopated* form of the same (beginning on the second half of the measure) from the first violin. The C sharp here is the crest of the emotional wave, whence it subsides first by the gradual descent of the motive through three octaves in measures 17–20, and then by the flagging of the accompaniment rhythm first to quarter notes, then to half notes. Still a different rhythm is heard in the last announcement by the first violin.

3. Harmonic. The harmony is absolutely the product of concurrent melodies throughout. No notes are added merely for color. Yet the sonorities, though effects rather than causes, are unforgettable.

4. Modulatory. The first measure strongly

establishes E major as the tonal center, and as the goal of what preceded the excerpt. A subtle change of the violin figure obscures the sense of tonality (by suggesting the atonal "whole-tone scale"), whereupon the first meditative version of the theme appears in the much darker key of A flat. The tonality is again clouded, and the theme appears once more in A, brighter than A flat, but less bright than the original E. The reappearance of this therefore, in the fifteenth measure, has the effect of an "*éclairissement*." The tonic of E major is maintained through the last eleven measures, giving a grateful sense of homecoming, of repose after adventure.

5. Instrumental. The student is referred to the score for detail. Particularly notable are the keenness of the violin E string at the moment of climax, and the earnest virility of the G string in the last statement.

III

The same loyalty to emotional truth that dictates all these processes of detail, guides also d'Indy's treatment of a composition considered as a whole. His conception of form, though set forth in the *Cours* in largely intellectual terms, can be thoroughly understood only when traced back to its emotional basis. Because for him a piece of music must hang together emotionally, must proceed, that is, all from a few ideas, and must evolve these freely and variously in obedience to the logic of emotion, he takes as his central principle Variation, or germination from root themes. Not only, he believes, should the single movement thus proceed from a few themes, but the entire work, according to what is called cyclic form, should result from their transformation and recombination. In other words, just as the rhythmic waxing and waning of the emotions embodied in a few themes gives rise to the single movement, the regarding of the same themes *from different points of view*, or under the domination of varying moods, will naturally generate the contrasted movements, all thematically related, of cyclic form.

It may at once be admitted that such a conception of form has its pitfalls. The same process that in the glow of creative emotion is a spontaneous reshaping of a theme to meet a new situation may in the absence of such emotion degenerate into a hammering of recalcitrant matter into mere distortion and ineptitude. That is what we note too often in Liszt's similar theme transformations in his symphonic poems, as when in "Les Préludes" he makes his love *cantabile* do reluctant duty as a trumpet call to war. D'Indy, let us confess it, is by no means guiltless on this score; in uninspired moments he becomes too easily the slave instead of the master of his process; living form stiffens into dead formula; and we have a more or less mechanical rearrangement of notes, as for instance that of the main theme of the finale in the B flat Symphony, based on the choral at the end, masquerading as a genuine reincarnation. Such scholastic passages do indeed appear as blemishes in too many even of his finest works. But it is fair to judge a process not by its occasional abuse, but by the possibilities a felicitous use of it opens up. These possibilities in the case of cyclic form are a maximum of diversity without diffuseness, and a maximum of unity without monotony or platitude.

That a development of something of the sort was indispensable to the progress of composition is evident when we reflect how intolerable literal recapitulation has become to the modern ear. Much of the prejudice against the sonata form in our day is due to the literal recapitulations of bunglers in the use of it. The remedy is, not to throw overboard the form, which is a natural, flexible, and convenient one, but to bring to it a freshness of feeling which penetrates at once to the spirit of it, ignoring the letter. Thus d'Indy, in the slow movement of the B flat Symphony, recapitulates the main theme, shown at Figure XXVI, *a*, not literally but in subtlest reincar-

FIGURE XXVI.

(*a*) Theme of slow movement, B flat Symphony. (This follows immediately after the introduction shown in Figure XX.)

(b) Return of theme in flute.

nation, one step higher in the scale, though still in the same key, and transferred from the sultry tones of clarinet, horn, English horn, and viola to the pure, pale sonority of a single flute, supported by lightest violin harmonies (Figure XXVI, *b*). It is the same theme, but breathing now a quite new sentiment.[1]

It is but a step from such a recreated recapitulation to a theme transformation such as we find in the last movement of the "Summer Day on the Mountain." This work is not only its composer's masterpiece in the sphere of program music; it is the latest and best of a whole series of works [2] in which he has expressed his love of his native country of the Cévennes in southeastern France. "At this moment," he once wrote in a letter from his château of Faugs, near Boffres in Ardèche, "I see the snowy summits of the Alps, the nearer mountains, the plain of the Rhone, the

---

[1] Compare, also, the theme of the Piano Sonata, in E minor, beginning with the note B, with the same theme altered, "*Mutatum*," in E major, beginning with G sharp.

[2] See for instance the "Poème des Montagnes," opus 15, for piano, and the Symphony on a Mountain Theme, opus 25, for piano and orchestra.

pine woods that I know so well, and the green, rich harvest which has not yet been gathered. It is a true pleasure to be here after the labors and the vexations of the winter. What they call at Paris 'the artistic world' seems afar off and a trifling thing. Here is true repose, here one feels at the true source of all art."

The "Jour d'Été à la Montagne," in three movements, "Aurore" ("Dawn"), "Jour — Après-midi sous les pins" ("Day : Afternoon under the Pines") and "Soir" ("Evening"), is characteristic of the composer in that, despite its program, there is in it little scene-painting, such as we find so constantly in Strauss and others. A memorable suggestion of dawn, with its vague shapes in the half-light and its bird songs, in the first movement[1]; a whiff of peasant dance-tune in the second, coming up through the baking heat under the pines; in the third some evening chimes from the valley: that is all. It is the emotional significance of the scene in its varying aspects,

---

[1] Note the progress from the dark key of C minor to the bright B major in "Dawn," reversed in "Evening," as another instance of the expressive use of modulation.

its appeal to the sympathies and associations of a poetic observer, that interest the musician. The main theme of the last movement (Figure XXVII, *a*) thus suggests the joy of life in the bright summer afternoon; its activity depicts no mere external scene, we feel, but reflects

FIGURE XXVII.

Finale of " Jour d'Été."

the elation of the sensitive heart, witnessing this scene. And when, at the end, after the suggestions of descending night and the distant jangle of chimes tempered by the evening air, the same melody returns in softest sonorities of strings and in quietest motion (Figure XXVII, *b*), we hear in it again no merely objective facts, but the tranquil evening thoughts of a poet, spiritualized in meditation. Never since he first essayed such theme transformation in a large work, in the "Symphony on a Mountain Theme" of 1886, which M. Paul Dukas called "a single piece in three episodes," has d'Indy been more successful in drawing

together the most opposing moods by the
single subjective point of view from which

Figure XXVIII.

(e) **Très lent**

they are regarded, as incarnated in a common theme. Never has he written a more characteristic page than that lovely breath of evening tenderness, the meditation of a lover on the world toward which darkness and sleep gently approach.

A work in which the cyclic method is applied with almost unparalleled rigor and resourcefulness, and which is therefore worthy of detailed analysis, is the String Quartet in E major,[1] built up from four notes of a Gregorian chant, shown at Figure XXV. The swinging main theme of the first movement, derived from this fragment by a natural rhythmic and tonal proliferation (see Figure XXVIII, *b*), is not immediately stated, but is rather anticipated tentatively, and gradually allowed to take shape, by a process dear to the composer, first through imitative bits for the different instruments and then through a serious fugato (Figure XXVIII, *a*). Once achieved it is broadly treated, with a richly conceived tonal digression into E flat major and return. A second theme, of sinuous curve and fluent movement (Figure XXVIII, *c*), is reached through a transition passage of more animated rhythm. The themes thus stated, development begins: not a perfunctory worrying of the themes such as the "free fantasia" often degenerates into in the hands of composers possessed of neither freedom nor fancy, but a

[1] The references are to the pocket edition of the score, published by Durand.

dynamic action and reaction of the themes such as d'Indy conceives development essentially to be. "Development," he says, "is . . . the action of the themes and ideas, and consequently their reason for being, since an idea is of value only through the action it is capable of exercising. When there are several ideas . . . the development expresses usually all the phases of a struggle between them, with the final triumph of one and submission of the other. . . . The themes comport themselves like living people : they act and move according to their tendencies, their sentiments, and their passions. These modifications show themselves both in the thematic elements which are elaborated as if to surpass themselves, or are restrained as if to become absorbed, and in the tonal trajectories which orient themselves toward light or toward darkness." [1] It will be seen that in this case the development first (pages 9 and 10) takes the aspect of a quiet presentation of the first theme in dark keys (E flat major, etc.) and then (from index number 10, through the whole of page 11) of

[1] *Cours de composition musicale*, Book II, Part I, pp. 241–242.

a brief recurrence of the second theme and elimination of it with the reviving force of the first, moving through more energetic rhythms and brighter tonalities to final victorious reassertion. The themes are then recapitulated and the movement ends with the beautiful coda we have already examined.

The two middle movements, too complex to analyze in detail, are based on themes strikingly illustrative of what was said a moment ago as to cyclic form arising from the approach to a common theme from different angles, or under the influence of varying moods. That of the scherzo is the theme envisaged playfully (Figure XXVIII, *d*); that of the slow movement (Figure XXVIII, *e*) shapes itself in response to a more serious contemplation. It may be pointed out that these are no mere clever or learned jugglings with notes, such as arise sometimes from the abuse of the method; not only are they true textually to the theme, but each is a faithful expression of its own mood; the resulting music accordingly convinces us emotionally as well as intellectually.

The finale is a piece of writing extraordinary

for the manifold resources developed out of the original theme, for the bold ingenuity of its polyphonic and rhythmic combinations, and for the variety of its emotional content. Its main theme comes from the original motive by *inversion* (Figure XXIX, *a*), and derives a

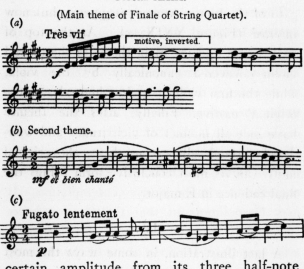

FIGURE XXIX.

(Main theme of Finale of String Quartet).

(*a*) Très vif

motive, inverted.

(*b*) Second theme.

mf et bien chanté

(*c*) Fugato lentement

certain amplitude from its three half-note rhythm proceeding deliberately against the more agitated two-four of other parts (especially the viola, at first, with a persistent figure taken also from the theme). Its second theme also traces its ancestry back to the first movement, but in a more elusive way; a comparison of Figure XXIX, *b*, with Figure XXVIII, *c*, will reveal the connection. The elaboration of these themes, and of the quaint staccato bridge passage between them, leads to most unexpected combinations. The fugato of the first movement reappears, but now *inverted* (Figure XXIX, *c*). At the top of page 58 we find the main theme in the second violin answered canonically by the viola, while the first violin sustains, high above, the original motive. Finally, after the themes have met all manner of vicissitudes and wandered through all sorts of keys, the original motive in its most conclusive form brings the final cadence in E major.

IV

A last illustration, in some ways the most striking of all, of d'Indy's conviction that emotional expressiveness is the criterion of the value of all artistic processes, is afforded by his attitude toward the peculiar idiom that has been developed by Debussy, Ravel, and others, and particularly toward the system of harmony based on the "whole-tone scale." His standpoint here is that of the open-minded and curious artist toward processes that may have new possibilities, saved from faddishness by a thorough familiarity with traditional resources and an indifference to novelty for mere novelty's sake. He has thus won the distinction of being blamed by the academic for "queerness," harshness, and obscurity, at the same time that he is patronized as reactionary by the "ultras."

The evidence of his works is that he makes free use of the whole-tone scale, as of all other technical elements, so far as it lends itself to the expression he has in mind, but no farther. There are already traces of it in certain passages of the early Clarinet Trio (1887) where he wishes to give a sense of groping uncertainty. In "Fervaal" (1895) its peculiar coloring is skilfully used in a number of passages, as, for example, that of the two bucklers, and its vigor and brilliancy, which so commended it to Moussorgsky in "Boris Godunoff," are exploited in the passage before the apparition of the cloud figures (see Figure XXX, *a*). In "Istar" a similar use is made of it for the calls which announce Istar's arrival at the different doors; to it is due a large measure of the mystical expression of the B flat Symphony, especially of the opening bass motive (Figure XXX, *b*) founded on the tritone which used to be regarded as "*diabolus in musica*," while the middle section of the scherzo draws upon its power of suspending the sense and piquing the musical curiosity (Figure XXX, *c*); in the opening of the piano

FIGURE XXX.

(*a*) From "Fervaal."

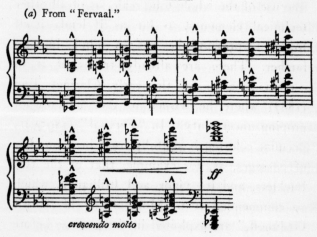

crescendo molto

(b) Opening of B flat Symphony

(c) Très animé

sonata splendid use is made of its clangorous sonorities.

But d'Indy is too sound an artist to lend himself to the abuse of any process, however fashionable, and he has the good sense to recognize the dangers of the whole-tone scale. In none of his critical writings has he expressed himself more courageously and at the same time more fairly, than in an article on "Good Sense"[1] in which he takes up this much-disputed matter.

"In the nineteenth century," he says, "some Russian composers, in the interest of certain

[1] "Le Bon Sens," *Revue Musicale*, S. I. M., November, 1912.

special effects, employed the scale of whole tones, which one may name atonal because it suppresses all possibility of modulation. In the twentieth century Claude Debussy and Maurice Ravel elaborated these methods, making often very ingenious applications of them; but they made the mistake (one must dare to speak the truth of those one esteems) of erecting processes into principles, or at least of letting them be so erected by their muftis, so that the formula now established by fashion is: 'Outside of harmonic sensation and the titillation of orchestral timbres there is no salvation.'

"This formula is dangerous, because far from constituting an advance it results in a retrogression of our art, and leads us backward by a hundred years. What these prophets try to establish is the rule of sense to the exclusion of sentiment, it is the supremacy of sensation over the equilibrium of the heart and the intelligence. This sensualist movement is neither new nor original. About a hundred years ago a similar aberration of good sense tried to poison our music. At the epoch of the Rossinis and the Donizettis the sensualist formula was 'All for and by melody!' To-day it is 'All for and by harmony!' I should say however that, of the two maladies, the second is less grave, for nothing is more ephemeral than new harmonies, if they do not take their point of departure from the two other elements of music: melody and rhythm. . . . In order that harmony should be durable, it must constitute, not mere glistening surface, mere tapestry, but rather the clothing of the living and acting being which is the *rhythmed melody*. The costume, in this case, may safely pass out of style — the human person, if it is well constituted, will endure.

"The scale of whole tones is far from being an improvement on our traditional occidental scale, since it suppresses all tonality and hence all modulation. Now, change of tonal place by modulation is one of the most precious elements of expression. To deprive oneself of it systematically is therefore a retrogression toward the barbaric monotony of past ages.

"What, then, does good sense demand? It demands very simple things — that the young composer should begin by learning his art, and should not allow himself to be hypnotized by a process that happens to be in fashion, employed fruitfully, to be sure, by certain natures, but not constituting in itself the whole of musical art.

"All processes are good, on condition that they never become the principal end, and are regarded only as means to make MUSIC."

The candor, courage, and penetration of such criticism as this, shown, though seldom in quite such measure, in every critical page that d'Indy has written, and the uncompromising nature of his views, not always free from narrowness, have of course made him many enemies. Probably no man in modern music is better loved or better hated. The devotion of his whole life to art, with a modesty, a suppression of self, a really religious enthusiasm rare in musicians, has naturally turned the love of his pupils and disciples into something that is almost worship; and this has in turn naturally enough irritated, sometimes to exasperation, those who vent their disgust of artistic idolatries on the often innocent idol, or who feel keenly, in a hero, the limitations of which no human being is free, or who find especially antipathetic, in M. d'Indy's case, certain temperamental leanings which he could not overcome if he would, such as those to conservatism, aristocracy, and even chauvinism in social relations, and to the strictest Roman Catholicism in religion.

Indeed, regarded simply as an intellect, d'Indy is something of a paradox, moments of the most penetrative insight alternating unaccountably in him with fits of prejudice or narrowness that suggest the existence upon his mental retina of incurable blind spots. What could be more illuminating in their unconventionality than such judgments as these, for example: — Of Schumann: "A genius in short and simple works, he finds himself lost when he has to build a musical monument. He then lets himself be guided by sentiment alone, and in spite of his often very fine ideas he can only *improvise* works of limited range, hasty fruits of an art not sufficiently conscious." Of Mendelssohn: — "Always skilful in appropriating the knowledge of others,

the Jews are seldom true artists by nature."
Of Grieg: "His short inspiration and his absolute ignorance of composition render him entirely inept in the construction of symphonic
works; he produces then only hybrid assem-
blages of short fragments, unskilfully welded
together or simply juxtaposed, without appearance of order or unity either in conception
or in execution." [1]   But the fastidiousness
already verging here on the finical seems always to be in danger, in dealing with subjects
on which he has active prejudices, such as
Jews, Protestants, free thinkers, and modern
Germans, of overshooting its mark, losing the
sense of proportion, and becoming narrowly
sectarian. Someone once said of him that
he had the spirit of the mediæval religious
fanatics, and had he lived in the Middle Ages
would have been burned at the stake for his
convictions, or would have burned others, as
the case might be, with equal ardor.

One thus catches sometimes a note of intol-
erance, almost of superstition, even in some
of his most valid judgments, putting one a

[1] *Cours*, Book I, Part II, pp. 406, 411, 419.

little on guard, perhaps rather by what is omitted or implied than by what is actually said. Thus Bach is great, "not because of, but in spite of, the dogmatic and withering spirit of the Reformation,"[1] and Franck's comment on Kant's "Critique of Pure Reason," that it was *très amusant*," is commended as one of the finest criticisms, "coming from the mouth of the believing French musician, that could be made of the heavy and undigested critique of the German philosopher."[2] Again "The present-day symphonists of Germany seem totally incapable of making anything great: they content themselves with making it big, which is not quite the same thing." They are charged with "total absence of artistic taste, misunderstanding of all proportion and of all tonal order."[3] They are "almost devoid of musical taste; they cannot distinguish good music from bad; the opinion of a German on a musical work has no importance."[4] The

[1] *Tribune de Saint-Gervais*, March, 1899.
[2] "Life of Franck," French edition, page 40.
[3] *Cours*, Book II, Part I, 487.
[4] *Revue Musicale*, December 1, 1906, quoted.

sympathy of the judicial with these pro-
nouncements wanes as they increase in ani-
mus; the justice of the first, to which any
thoughtful musician could hardly take exception, is obscured by the evident exaggeration of the last; and musical criticism too
evidently loses itself in chauvinism.

We need not concern ourselves here to estimate the exact proportion between wisdom
and prejudice in d'Indy's writings; the materials for a judgment have been admirably set
forth in Rolland's essay, and each reader
may judge for himself. The aim of these
citations is rather to illustrate the temperament of their author, and to show that in the
last analysis, even though these writings
make up perhaps the finest body of musical
criticism produced by a creative musician
since Schumann, that temperament is after all
originative rather than judicial. Much light
as there is in it, there is even more heat.
D'Indy is a crusader of beauty; the shining
spear is his natural weapon; and when he takes
to the clerk's ink-horn and balance sheet it is
always with a sort of youthful impatience.

He is essentially a poet, a maker; it is in his music that he finds his truest self. Indeed, he is too many-sided to be quite justly appreciated by his contemporaries; the poet has too much disappeared for us behind the teacher, the scholar, the critic, the philosopher, the devotee. On the occasion of the revival of "Fervaal" in 1913, M. Vuillermoz published an imaginary talk of this composite d'Indy to his adoring pupils, asking them not to idealize him, to let him remain human, to see in him the simple human lover, like his Fervaal, which he felt himself to be. It is time, for our own sakes, that we paid more attention than we do to this human lover that finds supreme expression in the Symphony in B flat, in "Istar," in the E major Quartet, in the "Jour d'Été à la Montagne." He it is who speaks to the young men, to his fellow lovers of immortal beauty, to the future. For, as one of his most understanding critics, Louis Laloy, has written of him: "Emotion is queen, and science is her servant." If d'Indy has studied as few modern musicians have studied, if he has drawn on the past for his ample means, it has been only in order to take more beauty with him, and to enable us to take it, into the future; and for all his intellectual power he has never forgotten that "Only the heart can engender beauty."

VI
MUSIC IN AMERICA
—

VI

MUSIC IN AMERICA

※

I

IN the discussions of "American music" that go on perennially in our newspapers and journals, now waxing in a wave of patriotic enthusiasm, now waning as popular attention is turned to something else, in war time much stimulated by an enhanced consciousness of nationality (unless indeed they are totally elbowed aside to make room for more immediate subjects), a sharp cleavage will usually be observed between those whose interest is primarily in the music for itself, wherever it comes from, and those in whom artistic considerations give way before patriotic ardor, and propaganda usurp the place of discrimination. One group, in uttering the challenging phrase, "American music," places the stress instinctively on the noun and regards the adjective as only qualification;

the other, in its preoccupation with "American," seems to take "music" rather for granted. Unfortunately the former group constitutes so small a minority, and expresses itself so soberly, that its wholesome insistence on the quality of the article itself is likely to be quite drowned out by the bawling of the advertisers, with their insistent slogan "Made in America." All the advantages of numbers, organization, and easy appeal to the man in the street are theirs. Even if we ignore those venal music journals which make a system of exploiting the patriotism of the undiscriminating for purely pecuniary purposes, there remain enough enthusiasts and propagandists, indisposed or unable to appraise quality for themselves, to create by their "booming" methods a formidable confusion in our standards of taste. Inasmuch, therefore, as we are condemned, for our sins, to be not only producers but consumers of this "American music," it behooves us to make careful inspection of the claims for it so extravagantly put forth, and to assure ourselves that we are getting something besides labels for our money.

What, then, is the precise value we ought justly to ascribe to that word "American" as applied to music, and wherein have those we may call champions of the adjective been inclined to exaggerate it? If we analyze their attitude, we shall find them the prey of two fallacies which constantly falsify their conclusions, and make them dangerous guides for those who have at heart the real interests of music in America. The first of these fallacies is that which confuses quantity with quality, and supposes that artistic excellence can be decided by vote of the majority. The second is that which identifies racial character with local idioms and tricks of speech rather than with a certain emotional and spiritual temper. Both lead straight to the oft-repeated conclusion that "ragtime" is the necessary basis of our native musical art.

Listen, for example, to one of the most persistent, courageous, and often interesting advocates of ragtime, Mr. H. K. Moderwell. "I can't help feeling," says Mr. Moderwell,[1] "that a person who doesn't open his heart

[1] The New Republic, October 16, 1915.

to ragtime somehow isn't human. Nine out of ten musicians, if caught unawares, will like this music until they remember that they shouldn't. What does this mean? Does it mean that ragtime is 'all very well in its place'? Rather that these musicians don't consider that place *theirs*. But that place, remember, is in the affections of some 10,000,000 or more Americans. Conservative estimates show that there are at least 50,000,000 copies of popular music sold in this country yearly and a goodly portion of it is in ragtime. . . . You may take it as certain that if many millions of people persist in liking something that has not been recognized by the schools, there is vitality in that thing." No doubt there is, just as by the same argument there is vitality in chewing gum and the comic supplements. The question is, of course, what sort of vitality? Yet if you raise this question of quality, you are immediately charged with being a "highbrow," "a person," in Professor Brander Matthews's already classic definition, "educated beyond his intelligence," — a charge from which any sane man naturally shrinks.

"The best American music is that which the greatest number of Americans like; the greatest number of Americans like ragtime; therefore ragtime is the best American music." This is a specious syllogism, which you may oppose only at the risk of being thought a highbrow and a snob.

Suppose, for instance, that you really do not happen to care for chewing gum, that just as a matter of fact, of personal taste, and not through any principles or sense of superiority to your fellows you prefer other forms of nutriment or exercise. You confess this peculiarity. Can you not hear the reproachful reply? "I can't help feeling that a person who doesn't open his heart to chewing gum somehow isn't human. Nine out of ten travelers on the subway, if caught unawares [with gum disguised as bonbons, let us say] will like it until they remember that they shouldn't. What does this mean? Does it mean that chewing gum is 'all very well in its place'? Rather that these punctilious people don't consider that place *theirs*. But that place, remember, is in the affections of

some 10,000,000 or more Americans. The
annual output of the chief chewing gum manu-
facturers"—etc., etc. Thus are you voted
down if you happen to be in the minority.
It does you no good to protest that you are
really quite sincere and without desire to
épater le bourgeois; that you can't help pre-
ferring Mr. Howells's novels to Mr. Robert
W. Chambers's, Mr. Ben Foster's landscapes
to Mr. Christy's magazine girls, Mr. Irwin's
"Nautical Lays of a Landsman" to the comic
supplements, and MacDowell's "To a Wild
Rose" to "Everybody's Doing It." If you
stray from the herd you must be sick. If you
vote for the losers you must be a snob.

Such charges are the more dangerous in
that they sometimes contain a half-truth.
There is a kind of person, the simon-pure snob,
who casts his vote for the loser just because he
is a loser, because he is unpopular, who prides
himself on his "exclusiveness," "excluding
himself," as Thoreau penetratively says,
"from all that is worth while." His is a sort
of inverted numericalism, based on quantity
just as essentially as the crude gospel of the

"10,000,000 or more Americans," but on quantity negative and vanishing towards the zero of perfect distinction. It is from his kind that are recruited the faddists, those who "dote on Debussy," the devotees of folksongs not for their human beauty but as curious specimens, those who invent all sorts of queer connections between music and painting or poetry, and indeed seem to find in it anything and everything but simple human feeling. It is not from these that we shall get any help towards the truth about ragtime. Indeed, they seem because of their unsympathetic attitude toward the spirit of music — its emotional expression — and their preoccupation with the letter of it, to be especially susceptible to the second fallacy of which we spoke — that of identifying racial quality with mere idiom rather than with fundamental temper.

Mr. Moderwell shall be spokesman of this view also. "You can't tell an American composer's 'art-song,'" he says, "from any mediocre art-song the world over. . . . You can distinguish American ragtime from the popular music of any nation and any age." Let us agree heartily that the mediocre "art-song" (horrid name for a desolating thing) is probably no better and no worse in our own than in other countries. Does this not seem an insufficient warrant for the excellence of types of art that can be more easily told apart? For purposes of labeling specimens earmarks are an advantage, but hardly for appraising modes of expression. If the important matter in American music is not its expression of the American temper, but the peculiar technical feature, the special kind of syncopation we call the "rag rhythm," then the important matter in Hungarian music is not its fire but its "sharp fourth step." Beethoven ceases to be Teutonic when he uses Irish cadences in his Seventh Symphony, and Chopin is Polish only in his mazurkas and polonaises. Of course this will not do; and Mr. Moderwell, to do him justice, after remarking that "ragtime is not merely syncopation — it is a certain sort of syncopation," adds "But of course this definition is not enough. Ragtime has its flavor that no definition can imprison." Our ultimate question is, then, not how many people like ragtime, or how few like it, or how easily can its idiom be told from other idioms, but how expressive is it of the American temper, how full an artistic utterance can it give of the best and widest American natures? This is a question not of quantity but of quality: of the quality of ragtime, the quality of America, and the adequacy of the one to the other.

II

Suppose, bearing in mind Mr. Moderwell's warning against snobbery, that "A Russian folk-song was no less scorned in the court of Catherine the Great than a ragtime song in our music studios to-day," we examine in some detail a typical example of ragtime such as "The Memphis Blues," of which he assures us that "In sheer melodic beauty, in the vividness of its characterization, in the deftness of its polyphony and structure, this song deserves to rank among the best of our time." [1] Here are the opening strains of it.

[1] "Two Views of Ragtime." The Seven Arts, July, 1917.

FIGURE XXXI.

From "The Memphis Blues."

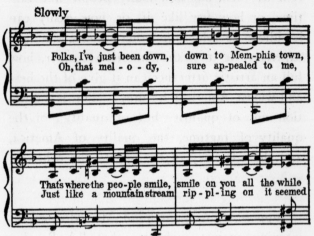

Approaching them with the eager expectation
that such praise naturally arouses, can we, as
candid lovers of music, find anything but
bitter disappointment in their trivial, poverty-
stricken, threadbare conventionality? How
many thousand times have we heard that
speciously cajoling descent of the first three
notes, that originally piquant but now indescribably boresome oscillation from the tonic
chord in the third measure? These are the
common snippets and tag-ends of harmony,

kicked about the very gutters, ground out
by every hurdy-gurdy, familiarity with which
breeds not affection but contempt. Their
very surface cleverness, as of meaningless
ornament, is a part of their offense. Russian folk-song indeed! Compare them with
the simple but noble tonic, dominant and
sub-dominant, of the "Volga Boat Song" and
their shoddiness stands self-revealed. And
the melody? Bits and snippets again, quite
without character if it were not for the rhythm,
and acquiring no momentum save in the lines
"I went out a-dancin'," etc., where they build
up well, but to a complete anticlimax in the
return of the obvious opening strain.

As for the rag rhythm itself, the sole distinctive feature of this music, it has undoubtedly something of real piquancy. The
trick, it will be noted, is a syncopation of half-
beats, arranged so as to pull bodily forward
certain comparatively strong accents, those
at the middle of the measures [1] — a scheme to
which words as well as melody conform. The
left hand meanwhile gives the regular metrical

---

[1] The time is really 4-8, though marked 2-4.

division of the measure, and a writer in the London Times, defining ragtime as "a strongly syncopated melody superimposed on a strictly regular accompaniment," points out that "it is the combination of these two rhythms that gives 'ragtime' its character." [1] This is perhaps not strictly true, since in some of the most effective bits of ragtime the metrical pulsation may give way momentarily to the syncopation, and everyone remembers those delightful times of complete silence in which the pulse is kept going mentally, to be finally confirmed by a crashing cadence. But it is usually the case that both time schemes, metrical and rhythmical, are maintained together. For this very reason we must question the contention of the champions of ragtime that its type of syncopation is capable of great variety, a contention in support of which some of them have even challenged comparison of it with the rhythmic vigors of Beethoven and Schumann. [2]

[1] The Times, London, February 8, 1913, quoted in Boston Symphony Orchestra Program Books, vol. 32, p. 1186.

[2] See, for instance, Mr. Carl van Vechten's "Interpreters and Interpretations."

The subtlety of syncopation as an artistic device results from its simultaneous maintenance of two time-patterns, the rhythmic and the metrical, in such a relation that the second and subordinate one, though never lost sight of, is never obtruded. The quasi-mechanical pulse of the meter is the indispensable background against which only can the freer oscillations of the rhythm outline themselves. The moment the sense of it is lost, as it is sometimes lost in those over-bold passages of Schumann where a displacement is too emphatically made or too long continued, the charm disappears. In the following from his "Faschingsschwank," for instance, the interest of the rhythmic accent on beat "three" lasts only so long as we oppose to it mentally a regular metric accent on "one."

FIGURE XXXII.

In the continuation of the passage, for which the reader is referred to the original, our minds are apt to "slip a stitch," so to speak, letting "three" and "one" coalesce. The moment this happens the passage becomes commonplace. But suppose, on the other hand, in the effort to maintain our sense of the meter, we strike the bass notes on each "one." Now equally, or indeed more than before, the charm is fled, and the passage rendered stale and unprofitable, through the actual presentation to the ear of so mechanical a reiteration. In short, the metrical scheme has to be mentally maintained, but actually, so far as possible, eliminated. Looking back, in the light of these considerations, at "The Memphis Blues," we shall realize that whatever the pleasing eccentricity of the rhythm, so relentless a meter as we here find thumped out by the left hand cannot but quickly grow tiresome, as indeed it will be felt to be after a few repetitions.

Reference to another well-known theme of Schumann will reveal a further weakness of ragtime. The second theme of the

finale of his Concerto for piano runs as follows:

FIGURE XXXIII.

Here the indescribably delightful effect is evidently due not only to the purely rhythmic
syncopation, but also to the fact that on the
silent strong beat of every second measure
harmony and melody as well as rhythm are so
to speak "tied up," or suspended, in such a
way that the syncopation is at the very heart
of the whole musical conception, and cannot
be omitted without annihilating the music.
Beside such essential syncopation as this the
mere pulling forward of certain notes, as in
"The Memphis Blues," is seen to be superficial, an arbitrary dislocation which may

disguise but cannot correct the triteness of the real melodic line. In fact, we seem here to have tracked ragtime to its lair and discovered what it really is. It is no creative process, like the syncopation of the masters, by which are struck forth new, vigorous, and self-sufficing forms. It is a rule of thumb for putting a "kink" into a tune that without such specious rehabilitation would be unbearable. It is not a new flavor, but a kind of curry or catsup strong enough to make the stale old dishes palatable to unfastidious appetites. Significant is it that, as the writer in the Times remarks, "In American slang to 'rag' a melody is to syncopate a normally regular time." The "rag" idiom can thus be put on and off like a mask; and in recent years we have seen thus grotesquely disguised, as the Mendelssohn Wedding March, for instance, in "No Wedding Bells for Me," many familiar melodies. To these it can give no new musical lineaments, but only distort the old ones as with St. Vitus' dance.

Thus the technical limitations of ragtime which we have tried to analyze are seen to be

in the last analysis the results and indices of a
more fundamental shortcoming — an emotional
superficiality and triviality peculiar to it.
Ragtime is the musical expression of an attitude toward life only too familiar to us all,
an attitude shallow, restless, avid of excitement, incapable of sustained attention, skim-
ming the surface of everything, finding nowhere
satisfaction, realization, or repose. It is a
meaningless stir-about, a commotion without purpose, an epilepsy simulating controlled
muscular action. It is the musical counter-
part of the sterile cleverness we find in so
much of our contemporary conversation, as
well as in our theater and our books. No
candid observer could deny the prominence in
our American life of this restlessness of which
ragtime is one expression. It is undoubtedly
what most strikes superficial observation. The
question is whether it is really representative
of the American temper as a whole, or is
prominent only as the froth is prominent
on a glass of beer. Mr. Moderwell thinks
the former: "I like to think," he says, "that
ragtime is the perfect expression of the Ameri-

can city, with its restless bustle and motion, its multitude of unrelated details, and its underlying rhythmic progress toward a vague somewhere." "As you walk up and down the streets of an American city you feel in its jerk and rattle a personality different from that of any European capital. . . . This is American. Ragtime, I believe, expresses it. It is to-day the one true American music."

To such an idolatry of precisely the most hideous, inhuman, and disheartening features in our national and musical life a lover of music and a lover of America can only reply that, first, it is possible that America lies less on the surface than we think, possible that it is no more adequately represented by Broadway than France is represented by the Parisian boulevards, or England by the London music halls; but that, second, if indeed the land of Lincoln and of Emerson has degenerated until nothing remains of it but "jerk and rattle," then we at least are free to repudiate the false patriotism of "My country, right or wrong," to insist that better than bad music is no music, and to let our beloved art subside finally under the clangor of subway gongs and automobile horns, dead but not dishonored.

III

That type of musical æsthetic which insists much on the importance of the racial and national differences dividing human kind into groups, and of the special features, technical and expressive, characterizing the music of these various groups, is constantly challenging our American music to disavow what it calls a featureless cosmopolitanism, and to achieve individuality by idealizing some primitive popular strain, whether of the Indians, of the negroes, of the British colonizers, or of our contemporary "ragtime." In so doing it usually accepts uncritically certain assumptions. It is apt to assume, for instance, that interpretative truth is assured by geographical propinquity. The chant of the Indian "expresses" the modern American because the habitat of both is west of the Atlantic Ocean. It often assumes that characteristic turns of idiom, such as certain modal intervals or rhythmic figures, are of intrinsic value as making music "distinctive." You can make a tune "American" by "ragging" its rhythm, as you make a story American by inserting "I guess" or "I reckon" at frequent intervals. It often mistakes the conception of the average for that of the ideal type, and supposes that the man in the street represents the best taste of America. Above all, it condemns any attempt at universalizing artistic utterance as "featureless cosmopolitanism" or "flabby eclecticism," and suggests that the musician who speaks, not a dialect but a language understood over the civilized world (as Tschaikowsky did, for example, to the disgust of the Russian nationalists), has "lost contact," as the phrase goes, "with the soil." In the interest of clear thinking all these assumptions stand in need of criticism.

It is hardly possible even to state the first without recognizing the large measure of absurdity it contains. That the crude wardances and chants of the red aborigines of this continent should be in any way representative of so mixed a people, compounded of so many

European strains, as we who have exterminated and displaced them, is a thought more worthy of savages who believe that the strength of their enemy passes into them when they eat him than of our vaunted intelligence, fortified by ethnological science. We should hardly entertain it if we were not misled by the interest that attaches to anything unusual or outlandish, and tempted by certain idiomatic peculiarities of these monotonous strains to exploit their "local color." This may very well be done now and then for an artistic holiday, as Mac-Dowell has done it in his Indian Suite; but if a folk-music is to enter vitally into art it must bring with it something more than quaintness or distinctive idioms, it must be genuinely expressive of the temperament of the people using it; and of the complex American temper Indian music can never be thus representative.

Somewhat similar considerations apply to the British folk-songs which, introduced by our pioneering grandfathers, have in remote regions like the Kentucky mountains survived uncontaminated by modernisms, and have recently been rediscovered and widely acclaimed. Here again the piquancy of unfamiliar idiom and a simplicity that falls agreeably on over-stimulated ears has aroused an enthusiasm that overshoots its mark. By all means let us enjoy these fresh songs, and even embody them in our music if we find it an interesting experiment. But can we expect that they will have any far-reaching interpretative value for us, that they will express our national temper? That they are not even native to the soil is a minor ob-jection to them, for we are importations our-selves. But that they are, with all their charm, British through and through, makes it unlikely that they can adequately reflect a nation which, though partly British, is also partly almost everything else.

The case of ragtime is rather more subtle. Here is a music, local and piquantly idiomatic, and undeniably representative of a certain aspect of American character — our restless-ness, our insatiable nervous activity, our thoughtless superficial "optimism," our fond-ness for "hustling," our carelessness of whither, how, or why we are moving if only we can "keep on the move." If this were all of us, if the first impression which foreigners get of us, summed up for them oftentimes in our inimitably characteristic "Step lively, please," were also the last, and there was nothing more solid, sweet, or wise in America than this galvanic twitching, then indeed ragtime would be our perfect music. But every true American knows that, on the contrary, this is not our virtue but our vice, not our strength but our weakness, and that such a picture of us as it presents is not a portrait but a caricature. And similarly, as soon as we examine ragtime at all critically we discover its essential triviality. Its melodies are commonplace, its harmonies cheap, shoddy, and sentimental. Even its rhythm, as we have seen, is a clever formula rather than a creative form, a trick for giving ordinary movement a specious air of animation. It is, in fact, as the writer in the London Times points out, "a debased imitation of genuine negro song, just as the popular Gaiety favorites of the late eighties, 'Enniscorthy' and 'Ballyhooley,' were debased imitations of a certain class of Irish folk-song." A few lines later this same writer falls into the pitfall always yawning for the theorist about ragtime, asks if the American composer will arrive who can extract gold from this ore, states coolly that "Ragtime represents the American nation," and of course ends up with an edifying reference to an art "really vital because it has its roots in its own soil." Does he consider that "Ballyhooley" "represents the Irish nation"? Would he advise Sir Charles Stanford to write a symphony upon it? Only an American journalist could be more naïve, and here is one that is. "The important point," he says, "is that ragtime, whether it be adjudged good or bad, is original with Americans — it is their own creation." [1] This beggars comment.

IV

So far our results are mainly negative. We have discovered fallacies in several assumptions too commonly and easily made. We have set a lower estimate on purely geographical considerations than is often set. We have

[1] Quoted by Mr. Charles L. Buchanan in an admirably sane article on "Rag Time and American Music" in The Opera Magazine, February, 1916.

tried to distinguish between what in a popular strain is merely quaint or piquant because of peculiarities of idiom, and what is more profoundly true in expression to a national or racial temper; and while admitting the superficial charm of such idioms and of the "distinctiveness" to which they minister, we have insisted on the far deeper import of interpretative truth. We have glanced at the danger of confounding appeal to the majority with appeal to good taste, which is always outvoted, or of supposing that "originality" is of any importance in comparison with merit. From these criticisms certain positive principles thus tend to emerge. It becomes evident that there is a certain gradation of values in the qualities which a folk-music may possess. Distinctiveness of idiom is a merit, but a less vital one than interpretative power; higher than either is beauty, suitability to enter into music that may bear comparison with the best music of the world. Is there any body of folk-song available to Americans that possesses any or all of these merits in a higher degree than the types we have examined?

We seem to discover such a richer vein in the songs of the negroes — not the debased forms found in ragtime and the "coon-songs" of the minstrel shows, but the genuine old plantation tunes, the "spirituals" and "shouts" of the slaves. In idiomatic individuality, to begin with, both of harmonic interval and rhythmic figure, these songs will compare favorably with those of any European nation. With many of these they share, indeed, odd modal intervals of great antiquity, such as the lowered seventh scale-step in major and the raised sixth-step in minor. Like Scottish tunes they make frequent use of the incomplete or pentatonic scale, omitting the fourth and seventh steps. A peculiarity in which they are almost unique is a curious oscillation between a major key and its relative minor, especially at cadences, so that one gets a haunting sense of uncertainty that enhances tenfold their plaintiveness. In "The Angels Done Changed My Name" (Figure XXXIV), are exemplified the lowered seventh step — at "I went to pray" — and the pentatonic scale; in "You May Bury Me in the East" the raised

FIGURE XXXIV.

The Angels Done Changed My Name. From "Jubilee Songs."

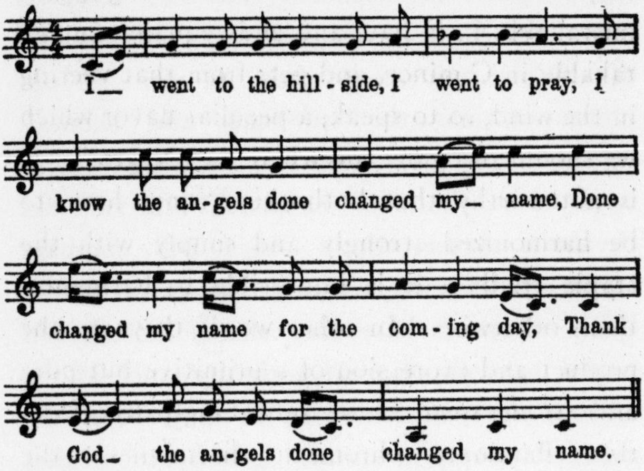

I went to the hill-side, I went to pray, I know the an-gels done changed my name, Done changed my name for the com-ing day, Thank God the an-gels done changed my name.

You May Bury Me in the East.

You may bu-ry me in the East, You may bu-ry me in the West, But I'll hear the trumpet sound in that morn-ing. In that morn-ing, my Lord How I long to go, For to hear the trumpet sound, In that morning.

sixth step — to the word "trumpet" — and the major-minor cadence. The last line begins unmistakably in E flat, and ends equally unmistakably in C minor, and gets from that veering in the wind, so to speak, a peculiar flavor which we should recognize anywhere as "Negro." It is noteworthy that both these songs have to be harmonized strongly and simply with the staple triads — it is impossible to harmonize them otherwise. In other words they are the product and expression of a primitive but pure and strong tonal sense, refreshingly free from the effeminate chromatic harmonies — the "barber-shop chords" — of ragtime. The one compares with the other as the fervent childish poetry of the lines here, "Thank God the angels done changed my name," or "I'll hear the trumpet sound in that morning" compares with the slangy doggerel of the cabarets.[1]

It is often stated that the chief rhythmic

---

[1] For example:

> "They got a fiddler there
> That always slickens his hair,
> An' folks he sure do pull some bow,"

from "The Memphis Blues," in which Mr. H. K. Moderwell assures us we shall find "characteristic verse of a high order."

characteristic of the negro music is the so-called
"Scotch jerk," the jump away from the normally
accented note to another, thrice exemplified
in the third line of "The Angels Done Changed
My Name," and imitated in ragtime. A more
typical instance of it is "Didn't My Lord
Deliver Daniel" (Figure XXXV), which also
further illustrates major-minor idiom in its
constant see-saw between G minor and B-flat
major. It is pointed out that the slaves had
a strong sense of time, that the overwhelming majority of their songs are in duple or
march time, with very few in the more graceful
but less vehement triple measure, and that in
their "shouts" or religious dances they rocked

FIGURE XXXV.

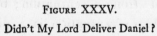

Didn't My Lord Deliver Daniel?

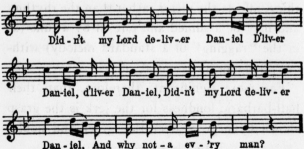

Did - n't my Lord de-liv-.er Dan-iel D'liv-er

Dan-iel, d'liv-er Dan-iel, Did-n't my Lord de-liv - er

Dan-iel, And why not-a ev - 'ry man?

Going Up.

Oh, yes, I'm going up, going up, going all the way, Lord, going up, going up, to see the hea-ven-ly land.

themselves into paroxysms of rhythmic excitement, one group clapping the meter while the others sang and scuffled with a "jerking, twitching motion which agitated the entire shouter and soon brought out streams of perspiration." [1] No doubt the jerk evidences their love of strong accentuation; but it must be noted that accentuation is a purely local thing, affects the meter rather than the rhythm, and may be assumed and put off by a tune (as in the "ragging" of a standard melody) without changing its essential curve.

Far more significant, therefore, than their half-barbaric fondness for the jerk is the grasp shown by negroes over the larger and nobler

[1] The Nation, May 30, 1867.

reaches of rhythm, their feeling for the phrase as a whole and ability to impress upon it a firm and yet varied profile. The second half of "You May Bury Me in the East," with its bold festooning of outline, even more strikingly the tune "Going Up," with its piquant silences and its even-paced insistence on "going all the way, Lord," show a unity in their variety, a certain "all-of-a-piece-ness," compared with which even "Didn't My Lord Deliver Daniel" seems scrappy, and the ordinary ragtime effusion pitifully poverty-stricken. There is plenty of internal evidence, too, that these happy results are attributable to genuine musical imagination, and not to luck in the servile following of felicitous word-patterns. Indeed, the frequency with which unimportant words are accented and important ones slurred over shows that, as is so often the case with great melodists like Schubert, the words were regarded more or less as convenient pegs to hang the melodies on, and the specifically musical faculty did not easily brook interference. "The negroes keep exquisite time," writes one of the editors of "Slave Songs in the United States," the best of the collections, "and do not suffer themselves to be daunted by any obstacle in the words. The most obstinate hymns they will force to do duty with any tune they please, and will dash heroically through a trochaic tune at the head of a column of iambs with wonderful skill." The sense of independent tone-pattern, which when possessed by individual geniuses in supreme degree gives us the immortal melodies of a Beethoven or a Brahms, waxes and wanes in these childlike tunes, sometimes falling back into platitude, but sometimes advancing to a real distinction and beauty.

Whether this beauty is of the kind we have desiderated as the highest quality folk-song can have, rendering it "suitable to enter into music that may bear comparison with the best music of the world," is a further question, and one which brings us at length to the highly controversial matter of the kind of treatment that the composer should give folk-material in incorporating it into his more finished art. The variations of taste concerned here are so subtle that probably unanimity of judgment,

even if it be desirable, will never be attained.
Yet it is certain that treatment of some sort
there must be. The mere collecting, collating,
and setting forth of folk-songs, attractively
arranged for instruments or even orchestrated,
such as we have seen much of from all countries
in recent years, is no more musical art than a
pile of bricks is a building, or a series of anec-
dotes literature. So far as it tends to content
the public with such potpourris, the fad for
folk-song is positively injurious to taste, in
something the same way that our modern
floods of petty journalism are injurious to the
capacity for sustained reading. Moreover, even
on their own level such medleys are apt to be
unsatisfactory; for the tunes themselves are
so definite, brief, and complete, and the transitional passages between them are therefore so
obtrusively transitional, that the net effect
is that of the ill-baked bread pudding from
which we eat nothing but the raisins. Mr.
Coleridge-Taylor's "Twenty-Four Negro Melodies," despite incidental attractions, are on
the whole an example of this bad model.

Far worse, however, are those "improvements" of folk-song which consist in a general prettifying of its homely simplicity with all the refinements and luxuries of sophisticated musical technique — as if a country maiden should conceal her healthy color under layers of rouge. Strange that composers skilful enough to use them should not recognize the inappropriateness of Wagnerian chromatics and Debussyan whole-tone scale harmonies, to say nothing of all sorts of rich dissonantal trappings, to tunes as diatonic as "God Save the King" and as square cut as the "Hymn of Joy." One would think that the sense of humor, which revels in incongruity in music as in other things, would keep them from doing it and us from taking it so seriously. It would be invidious to name examples, but they can be discovered by the discerning; for not even the negro complexion is proof against this brand of talcum powder.

The kind of change that is both legitimate and necessary may perhaps be best suggested by another example, "Deep River." Here we have, in the first phrase, that free and firm molding of rhythmic pattern which is often

FIGURE XXXVI.

Deep River.

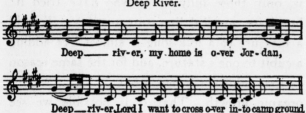

Deep—— riv-er, my home is o-ver Jor-dan,

Deep—riv-er,Lord I want to cross o-ver in-to camp ground.

so surprising in these songs, so that we might look far in the best composers without finding its peer in deliberate, calm beauty. But just as our hearts are responding to the wave of emotion thus generated it strikes, so to speak, a dead wall, falls shattered, and has to begin over again, without being able to recover the lost momentum. The imagination is vital as far as it goes, but its span is short, it lacks sustained power and cumulative force. What is needed in the composer who would deal with such material, then, in addition to a tact that enters into its spirit, is a synthetic imagination capable of rounding out its incompleteness, of tracing the whole of the curve it suggests, of developing into full life what it presents only as a germ.

How difficult such a truly creative treatment is, only those fully know who have tried it; how rare, musical literature testifies. To add a measure to a folk-song is almost like adding a cubit to one's stature, and for the same reason — that addition is not what is requisite, but organic growth. That it is possible we see in Brahms's masterly treatment of German student songs in his "Academic Festival Overture"; that it can be applied to negro melodies we have been shown especially by Dvořák. In his "New World" symphony and his "American" Quartet and Quintet he assimilated a peculiar idiom so perfectly that there is not a note, even in the highly complex harmonies toward the end of the symphony, that does not take its place in the scheme unobtrusively. While the harmonic idiom preponderantly of simple triads dictated by the material is maintained with an unerring sense of style, these commonest of all chords are so deftly managed that they never become commonplace. The twin pitfalls of platitude and sophistication are avoided with equal success. The same felicity is attained in the construction. However brief the themes, they do not sound trivial or unconvincing, because we feel they have reached their natural growth. Above all, the same sympathy and power that are shown in these technical matters so control the conception as a whole that these works form a true idealization of negro feeling, in its moods both of half-barbaric dance and of naïvely pathetic sentiment.

Dvořák's example suffices by itself, then, to show that the negro music, in the hands of a master, is capable of two of the three qualities we demanded of any folk-song — idiomatic distinctiveness and capacity for organized beauty. Does he also demonstrate in it the third — adequacy to interpret the American temper? Something closely kindred to that temper and easily endeared to it there certainly is in the restless rhythmic energy, the unceasing motion and quick changes of these scherzos, the vigor and dispatch of these allegro movements. Like similar syncopations and other rhythmic peculiarities that we find in those of our composers who have more than their share of our national nervous energy, such as Chadwick and Whiting, the negro rhythms have a crispness and buoyancy that is somehow appropriate to our clear skies and self-helpful society. They give at least a far fairer portrait of us than the caricature of ragtime. In its more sentimental moods, too, negro music has an unsophistication, an unreserved naïveté, that reminds us of similar traits in the traditional conception of our fellow countrymen. It thus seems to express more of our national temperament, and to leave less of it unexpressed than would on the whole any other body of folk-song.

Yet the very attempt to formulate these considerations forces us to realize how hopelessly inadequate they are as an account of the possibilities of America in music. The picture they give of the national type may do something like justice to it as it existed in earlier times and simpler surroundings, as it appears, for instance, in the pages of Mark Twain or Bret Harte, and as it is symbolised in the person of Uncle Sam; but the modern American is a being quite other, far more complex, far more cosmopolitan, the American not of nineteenth century New England but of the twentieth century "melting pot." He is wholly incommensurate not only with negro music or any folk music, but with even individual composers like Dvořák in whom emotion far outruns intellectual subtlety. No folk music, let us repeat, no individual composer, no school of composers, can "express" America. The age of such simplicities is past, if it ever existed. Whether we like it or not, we have to take our age and our country as they are; they are an age of rapidly accelerating intercommunication of all peoples and a country in which the internationalism that thus slowly results is being hastened by actual admixture on a heretofore unprecedented scale. Such a condition doubtless has its bad as well as its good aspects; but if those who bemoan our "featureless cosmopolitanism" and advocate an impossible parochialism as the only remedy would try rather to see how a wider outlook and a larger sympathy may deepen our art and make it more truly human by laying less stress on local, national, or even racial types, and more on the untrammeled expression of the greatest possible variety of individuals, music would fare better. "National literature:" wrote Goethe to Eckerman in 1827, "the term has no longer much meaning to-day; the time for universal literature is come, and each ought to work to hasten its advent." Signs are not wanting that the condition thus discerned by the wisest men a century ago is now gradually getting itself acknowledged in general practice.

V

If we accept, in the light of the foregoing considerations, the ideal of enlightened eclecticism, not only for our own music here in America but measurably for all modern music, since it is all subject to the internationalization so characteristic of our time, the chief undertaking that remains to us will be an attempt to define the position of the American composer in relation to such eclecticism, the advantages and disadvantages of his situation, the pitfalls he must avoid, and the opportunities he should embrace. From this point of view it will be seen that the enthusiasts of nationalism, in advising our composer to confine himself to Indian, Negro, or ragtime material, in adjuring him not to listen to the siren voice of Europe, are not merely misleading but cheating him. They are asking him to throw away his birthright of wide cosmopolitan influence for a mess of purely parochial pottage. They are bewailing the lack in America of just those geographical and racial boundary lines that split up Europe into a series of more or less petty and hostile camps. They are inviting us to descend from the point of vantage good fortune has given us, a little removed both in space and in time from the thick of the battle.

For it is indeed the peculiar good fortune of the young American composer that he finds spread out before him, as the models through the study of which he is to acquire an important part of his technical equipment and of his general attitude towards art, the masterpieces of the various European countries, among which he may pick and choose as his individual taste directs, and without being hampered by those annoying racial and national jealousies from which the most intelligent European cannot quite free himself. What he may acquire of the special virtue of each school — the delicacy and distinction of the French, the solid structural power of the German, the suave and rich coloring of the Russian, the austere dignity of the English — is limited, not by the accident of birth, but only by his own assimilative power. No element in his complex nature need be starved for want of its proper food. He is placed in the midst of the stream of world influences to make of himself what he will and can.

Is it not inconceivable that one thus privileged to speak, within the measure of his ability, a world language should ever content himself with a Negro or Indian dialect? It would be so perhaps did we not consider that, in order to speak the world language of cosmopolitan music as it exists to-day, one must spend years in laborious discipline and in obscurity, while any tyro can make a certain effect and gain a certain prominence by stammering in an idiom strongly enough tinctured with local color. Vanity is the immemorial enemy of art; if the itch to be conspicuous once infect him, the artist forgets all those subtle adaptations, those difficult reconcilements, which were formerly his passion, and makes a crude effect that appeals much more to the primitive minds of the masses. And this he may do quite unconsciously and in the sincere belief that he is pursuing the highest ideals. In the presence of the immediate good, of recognition and acclaim, it is pitifully easy to forget the remote better, the broader, finer, subtler beauty that is not yet understood.

But if the picturesque, the quaint, the piquant, is by nature more quick to appeal than the beautiful, it is also more short-lived. For this reason those writers in all ages and countries who depend largely on local color are promptly acclaimed and soon forgotten, while those who aim at the more universal human qualities win gradually a place that proves permanent. Bret Harte was doubtless considered more "American" by his own generation than Emerson. Shakespeare is far less English than Defoe, Dante is not so notably Italian, or Goethe so notably German, as are many lesser men. Or, to come back to music, where are now the Russian "nationalists" who excluded Tschaikowsky the "cosmopolite" from their magic circle? For a while we listened to their melancholy Russian cadences with fascinated interest, in spite of their crude harmonization, their incoherent form, their lack of instinct for style, because we were pleased with the novelty. Now the novelty has worn off, and for human nature's daily food we find Tschaikowsky, who made the most of his opportunities, rose above a narrow exclusiveness, and assimilated power wherever he found it, far preferable.

The true difficulty of the American composer's position, then, is to be found, not in the poverty of the native folk-song, but in the confusing variety of the foreign influences in which he is so rich. He has suffered and is still suffering from an embarrassment of riches, from a mental indigestion. His cosmopolitanism is indeed too often "featureless," and his readiness to be influenced an evidence of weakness rather than strength, a flat rather than a broad eclecticism. His technique is miscellaneous, his style without distinction, his art as a whole lacks individuality. This featurelessness is the typical defect of American compositions of the present generation, perhaps — typical in spite of some notable exceptions. The technical deficiencies of our pioneer forefathers are more and more becoming things of the past; free intercourse with Europe and the wholesale importation of skilled European musicians have refined away the crudities with surprising rapidity; there are among us to-day musical workmen whose skill in symphony, chamber music, and opera will compare favorably with that of Europeans. Where we still fail is in that subtle, indefinable, and indispensable touch of personal distinction which may be recognized in artists so diverse, both individually and racially, as Strauss, d'Indy, Debussy, Rachmaninoff, Paderewski, Sibelius, Elgar. What is the secret of this distinction?

We may get a clue to the right answer by considering a peculiar case, an exceptional case, among ourselves — the exception that proves the rule — the case of MacDowell.

The supreme place he undoubtedly holds among our composers is due precisely to this quality of personal distinction, of individuality, to the fact that his music, in spite of the pronounced Grieg and Raff elements in it, does not sound quite like that of any one else. Technically MacDowell has grave deficiencies; his harmonic system is singularly limited, mannered, and monotonous; his polyphony is weak; his "drawing," as a painter would say, is often halting and awkward. His range of expression, moreover, is not wide, and within it he frequently cloys by an over-sweet sentimentalism. But MacDowell is sincere, and he is always himself. There are no unfused elements in his style, no outstanding features, that we feel to have been borrowed and not assimilated. His style is very narrow, but it is his own. And the result is that, although we shall soon forget some of our composers who are far cleverer than he, we shall not forget MacDowell.

The enemies of eclecticism have thus expressed a half-truth, we begin to see, when they call it flabby. Only too easily does it become so. As dangerous as it is desirable, it will contribute to the formation of an artist only when it is controlled by an instinctive sense of how much one can assimilate, and the courage to reject the rest. And here we come to one of those peculiar difficulties of the position in which the American composer finds himself. It is hard for him, recognizing, as his natural alertness of perception and his detached point of view enable him to do, the merits of many different European aims and methods, and, mainly sensitive as he must be to his own shortcomings in respect to any of them — it is hard for him to distinguish between those that he can possibly assimilate to his own uses and those that must remain alien to him; and it is doubly hard to let the latter alone, voluntarily restricting his field in order that he may be the master of it. Yet these selections, these sacrifices, are at the very foundation of artistic personality. It is no more possible for a human being to be, let us say, at once as subtle as Debussy and as gorgeous as Strauss than it is to be in two places at once. Which will you do without? But the young American composer is at once too timid and too ambitious to do without anything; in the attempt to be everywhere at the same time he cuts himself up into little pieces that end by being nowhere.

The frank and courageous acceptance of limitations is, in truth, the first step toward artistic individuality; a man can never be an individual, as the very derivation of the word may remind him, so long as he remains divided, spread out very wide and very thin, unwilling to take sides, but only when he concentrates himself, is loyal to one cause, grows out from one nucleus. What this nucleus shall be, indeed, differs according to circumstances. For the European musician it is to some extent decided beforehand, by the conditions of birth, of national and racial allegiance. The American, as we said, to begin with is freer in this respect; but we may now add that he is no less bound to find a cause, a unifying center, if he would get beyond mere clever imitation and become a genuine person. He must love his cause so singly that he will cleave to it, and forsake all else. Now what is this cause for the American composer but the utmost musical beauty that he, as an individual man with his own qualities and defects, is capable of understanding and striving towards? And what is the "all else" that he must forsake, save those types of musical beauty which, whatever may be their intrinsic worth, do not come home to him, do not arouse a sympathetic vibration in him, leave him cold? He must take sides. He must be, not a philosopher, but a partisan. He must have good hearty enthusiasms, and good hearty prejudices. Only so can he be an individual.

It matters not one jot, provided this course of personal loyalty to a cause be steadfastly pursued, what the special characteristics of style of the music may be to which one gives one's devotion. Let A give his life to studying the delicate color scheme of the French "ultra-moderns"; let B find his joy in a polyphony based on Bach's; let C develop lovingly the cadences or rhythms of Negro and Indian tunes; all three will be good musicians, all three good Americans — for, after all, American music is only music. The man who is neither good musician nor good American is the botcher, the dilettante, the clever amateur — he who is too lazy to learn his business, too pretentious to limit his claims, too busy talking about art to study it. Such babblers have always been, and always will be, naturally, far more numerous than the efficient workers; and they will doubtless continue to fill the newspapers and magazines with their silly superficialities, and do their utmost to confuse the public into forgetting that sincerity and skill are the only things that can ever be justly demanded of an artist.

VI

In demanding skill and sincerity of our composers, however, we are requiring of them, as a little analysis will suffice to show, labors and sacrifices of which only the rarest natures are capable; and it may well be that the unsatisfactory character of composition in America is due far more to the rarity of men able or willing to undertake such labors and endure such sacrifices than to the difficulties of the æsthetic problems we have so far been considering. Let us, then, in closing, try to suggest answers to the purely practical questions : Is there anything about our social and economic system that lays especial burdens on creative artists? If there is, is there any hope of correcting it? Whether it may be corrected or not, may our composers, through candid recognition of it, be saved from dissipation of energy and helped to concentrate their efforts on objects most likely to be achieved, and most worth achieving? We shall answer all these questions affirmatively.

First we must note that the amount and intensity of mental application involved in composition is something of which the layman has little idea. The technique to be mastered by the composer is singularly difficult; the tonal material he works in is subtle and intangible; its relationships, harmonic, rhythmic, melodic, polyphonic, which he must learn not only to understand but to manipulate, are of an indescribable complexity; and he achieves command of all these fundamental or grammatical means of his art only to face the far subtler distinctions of structure and style on a wise apprehension of which depends his artistic individuality. Moreover, if he would take advantage of the wide and unbiased view of European music which we have seen to be a special privilege of the intelligent American, he must do far more than hear or read the chief works of many masters; he must know them in and out, must learn to breathe the peculiar atmosphere of each, — must, in short, live with them. And more than that, for after analysis comes synthesis, after assimilation, creation; and as the one requires laborious, minute, detailed study, the other requires a wide margin of leisure in which the mind can forget all these details, empty itself of all irrelevance, and prepare to receive whatever thoughts may visit it. Here is more time needed, in great spaces. This is a full and varied way of living, indeed, that we are sketching; and we have not yet made out how the artist is to live at all. How is he to get money to support himself?

Not, certainly, from his compositions. They will do well if they bring him enough to pay for ink and paper; they will surely not pay for their own copying. "A man," says Mr. Graham Wallas,[1] "who gives the best strength of each day to dreaming about the nature of God or the State, or the shape of the earth, or the relation of the sides of a triangle to its hypotenuse, produces nothing which at the end of the day he can easily sell. Since the actual process of inference is unconscious, and his voluntary control over it indirect and uncertain, he is not even sure that he will produce any result at all, whether salable or unsalable, by months of effort. How then shall he live?" If this is the situation of the creative thinker in science, what shall we say of that of the creative thinker in art? As we have seen in discussing the relations of democracy and music, the class which in the eighteenth century bought the wares of the composer finds its analogue, under our capitalistic industrial system, in the frivolous plutocracy, who demand of music curiosities, novelties, and entertainment. The vast mass of listeners emerging from below, on the other hand, of crude and

---

[1] "The Great Society," by Graham Wallas.

childlike taste, prefer stories (program music), day-dreaming, and sensationalism to beauty. Confronted by these two classes, the composer will find his sincerity likely to cost him dear. If he is really sincere, if he is trying to write music that presents the kind of beauty that he hears, and that no one else has heard in just that way before, he will find himself enjoying it in a minority of one. Yet the alternative, to prostitute himself and "give the public what it wants," is even worse; and when the public says to him, in the words of Mozart's publisher, "Write in a more easy, popular style, or I will not print a note or give you a kreuzer," his answer can be no other than Mozart's: "Then, my good sir, I have only to resign myself and die of hunger."

Or rather, and here is the special irony of the situation, his alternative is not a literal physical hunger, but that subtler hunger that follows the denial of the imperious instinct to create beauty; he has not to starve his body of bread, but his soul of music. For while society withholds with one hand, so to speak, any payment for the best work he can do, because it is too good, because it requires too long to be understood, it freely offers him with the other a bare livelihood, if not more, for work of secondary value — teaching, performance, exposition, anything but creation. It constantly pulls, pushes, cajoles, persuades, coaxes, browbeats him from the superior to the inferior activity. It so fills his days with the one that even if at long intervals an opportunity for the other presents itself he has hardly the spirit to seize it. It deadens him with detail, drugs him with drudgery, cages him until he forgets how to sing. Where, as in America, there exists a very "high standard of living," as it is quaintly called, meaning that many and costly material wants have to be met before spiritual needs can be considered, the labor imposed by such a struggle may be overwhelming. And it is superimposed, we must remember, on the other labor, the creative one, described above. The same nerves, body, and brain, in the same twenty-four hours each day, must sustain the two labors, one to earn a livelihood, the other to make use of it. No wonder few can endure it; no wonder most give it up in despair or dull indifference, and content themselves with the livelihood without taking the trouble to live.

Not only, moreover, are the broad facts of economics, under a capitalistic-industrial system, thus flatly inimical to creative work, but in a plutocratic civilization like ours the more subtle forces of public opinion are perhaps even more fatal to it, because more pervasive and intangible. In Europe the impecunious artist is accepted with tolerance, even with a touch of respect, and suffered to live undisturbed in his Bohemia and to pursue his dreams. To us, who still as a people recognize no measure of achievement but income, and who accept without a murmur the domination of mass-convention in most matters of opinion, he is something worse than an interesting eccentric or even a harmless crank; he is something of a sybarite and a skulker; he is one who "doesn't play the game." Therefore he need look to us for understanding or sympathy no more than for more material rewards. If he wishes to be approved of, let him do something useful — that is, something that pays.

When we realize the penalties that are thus
piled upon the head of the artist whose only
offense is that he wishes to give something to
society of which it does not yet recognize the
value, our wonder that there is so little American composition of the first quality changes
to surprise that there is any. We begin to
suspect — as Ruskin did at forty, and devoted
the rest of his life to demonstrating the truth
of his suspicion — that the decadence of art
we witness all around us is only a symptom of
a deeper disease, and that, as William Morris
expressed it, "Slavery lies between us and
art." [1] Capitalistic industrialism, as Matthew
Arnold saw, "materializes our upper class,
vulgarizes our middle class, brutalizes our
lower class"; and under such conditions vital
art can have no secure or assured life. It
may well be, therefore, that art can only in the
long run be saved, like society itself, by the
fairer, freer, humaner system that socialism
promises. It cannot but thrill all true lovers
of art to find its claims, with those of a liberal-

[1] Quoted in "The Socialist Movement," by J. Ramsay Mac-
Donald, p. 86.

ized society, being championed to-day, no longer merely by individual thinkers like Ruskin and Morris, but by great representative bodies like the British Labor Party. "Society, like the individual," says a draft report of this party [1] "does not live by bread alone — does not exist only for perpetual wealth production. The Labour Party will insist on greatly increased public provision being made for scientific investigation and original research, in every branch of knowledge, not to say also for the promotion of music, literature, and fine art, which have been under capitalism so greatly neglected, and upon which, so the Labour Party holds, any real development of civilization fundamentally depends."

Finally, however, inspiring as are the hopes these words suggest, the American composer need not await their realization before putting forth those individual efforts without the aid of which, after all, they can never attain it. Music, like society, has reached its present

[1] The Labor Party's Draft Report on Reconstruction: "The Aims of Labour," by Arthur Henderson, Appendix, page 106.

state only through the struggles, against immense odds, of its martyrs and its heroes: not only of Bach, of Mozart, of Beethoven, of Schubert, of Wagner, of Brahms, but of countless others who have wrought and suffered in obscurity and with a consecration of their more limited powers to the great cause of beauty. And if American life lays almost crushing burdens on artistic initiative, there is also in the best American tradition a courage, an independence, a certain nonchalant and plucky self-reliance that ought to carry an artist far on the solitary path he has to travel. It ought to keep him from turning back, though it could not guard him against wandering and getting lost. All that can help him there is clearsightedness, a realistic and unsentimental view of the society in which he lives and the terms on which he lives in it. He must discharge the work he does for a livelihood as conscientiously as he can, but meanwhile not forget to live also. He must not make the tragic mistake, the unpardonable sin of the artist, described by Thoreau: "To please our friends and relatives we turn out our silver ore in cartloads, while we neglect to work our mines of gold known only to ourselves, far up in the Sierras, where we pulled up a bush in our mountain walk, and saw the glittering treasure. Let us return thither. Let it be the price of our freedom to make that known." He must cut down his material requirements to the minimum and honor his own poverty. He must learn to find his satisfaction in the work itself, and not expect recognition, which is bound to be late (even later in America than elsewhere), and likely to be mistaken. Above all, he must not pity himself or grow embittered, for in the possession of a lifelong enthusiasm, an ideal that he can always work towards and will never reach, he has the best gift that life has to offer.

Printed in the United States of America.